MW00910423

The Revolution Revisited:

Effective Schools and Systemic Reform

by
Barbara O. Taylor
and
Pamela Bullard

Phi Delta Kappa Educational Foundation
Bloomington, Indiana

Cover design by
Victoria Voelker

Library of Congress Catalog Number 95-71480
ISBN 0-87367-483-9
Copyright © 1995 by Barbara O. Taylor and Pamela Bullard
Bloomington, Indiana

*This book is dedicated
to the thousands of courageous practitioners,
trainers, facilitators, students, and citizens
who have unselfishly persevered
in the quest for public school reform.*

Table of Contents

Introduction 1
   Using the Effective Schools Process 2

Chapter 1: Effective Schools Defined 7
   The Correlates 9
   The Process 11
   The Vision 14
   The Promise 15
   Effective Schools and Total Quality 21
   Learning to Ride a Unicycle 24

Chapter 2: Development of the Effective
   Schools Process 27
   Roots of Effective Schools Research 28
   Sticking to the Goal 31
   Refining the Model 33
   NCESRD Moves to Wisconsin 37

Chapter 3: Changing the Classroom 41
   Reasons for Change 41
   The Power of Moral Imperative 45
   The Role of Brain-Compatible Learning 46
   Bringing Brain-Compatible Learning to the
      Spring Branch Effective Schools Process 49
   Empowerment and Learning 52

Chapter 4: Changing the Culture of Schools 57
   Shared Values, Shared Vision 58
   Effective Schools and Other Reforms 60
   Stages of Culture Change 65
   Making Change Stick 67

Chapter 5: Curriculum Development, Student Assessment, Staff Development, and Accountability 71
The Fallacy of "Loose Coupling" 73
Collaboration, Consensus, and Group Learning 75
Collaboration in Action in Spring Branch 76
Measuring Results 77

Chapter 6: Effective Leaders and What They Do: Four Cases 81
The Spring Branch, Texas, Experience 81
Change in St. John's County, Florida 86
Transformations in Springfield, Massachusetts 93
20 Years of Effective Schools in Arizona 96
Conclusion 103

Chapter 7: Facing the Future: How Effective Schools Meet the Challenges 105
The Danger of the Bell Curve 108
Toward a New Stewardship 111

References 117

About the Authors 121

Introduction

Why is an update on Effective Schools needed now?

The answer is simple. Pundits still pontificate about what is needed to make American schools effective, competitive, and "world-class." Gurus still grouse that little progress has been made in public school reform. Politicians still polarize communities around education issues. But in schools across the nation, thoughtful practitioners — quietly and successfully — have been working on a process of school reform known as Effective Schools.*

Beginning in 1977 in Pontiac, Michigan, and then in 1978, three demonstration projects began the hard work of applying the tenets of Effective Schools to real schools in real districts. These demonstration projects were the Pontiac Project, the School Improvement Project in New York City, and Rising to Individual Scholastic Excellence (RISE) in Milwaukee. Now, in 1995, enough has been demonstrated, enough documented, and enough accomplished by practitioners to declare that the Effective Schools Process makes it possible to structure (or restructure) schools and districts so that all children learn the intended curriculum.

In a field where the top rewards go to university researchers who coin new names for old concepts and then disseminate their "flavor of the month" by making speeches, those practitioners who have worked out the Effective Schools Process run the risk of being marginalized because, well, "isn't Effective Schools old hat?" The answer is a resounding "No!" Public school practitioners understand that merely making speeches about "new" discoveries does not result in school reform. Effective Schools Research

---

*The words *Effective Schools, Effective Schools Research*, and *Effective Schools Process* are capitalized to denote a specific body of work developed and espoused by the National Center for Effective Schools Research and Development (NCESRD) at the University of Wisconsin-Madison. Effective Schools, Effective Schools Research, and Effective Schools Process are service marks (SM) of NCESRD.

1

must be applied to be useful, and then the Effective Schools Process must be disseminated through coordinated staff development and program implementation. Agile, pragmatic minds working in the field, not pundits and gurus, make school reform happen.

Schools in more than 700 districts nationwide are now working to become Effective Schools. These practitioners are committed to staff development in new classroom methods, to peer coaching, to new forms of assessment, and to the continuous refinement of their art. Making reform happen is hard work undertaken daily, and the results are documented and evaluated through action research by those actively at work in the schools.

So what is the Effective Schools Process today?

A basic tenet of Effective Schools is that all children can master the basic skills needed to be successful in school. The ideal of equity imbedded in the Elementary and Secondary Education Act of 1965 was translated into real practices by the early Effective Schools researchers. But they did not accept the concurrent notions of supplementary education (Title I) or tracking, holding instead to the precept that true equity can be achieved only when classroom teachers are trained and held accountable for teaching *all* students.

Today, the twin notions of "equity" and "excellence" strongly drive the school reform movement. Teaching all children the intended curriculum — once a revolutionary statement — is now the accepted goal of education.

Using the Effective Schools Process

The Effective Schools Process is a change process that can be used at all levels of education to restructure and reorganize schools, districts, and even state boards of education to focus on one overriding goal: All children will learn the intended curriculum to a high standard. The Effective Schools Process makes this renewal possible by enabling and empowering principals, parents, and classroom teachers and by providing coordinated professional development. School people and community representatives are shown how to go about the work of restructuring schools by actually doing the tasks that need to be done under the guidance of trainers and facilitators who themselves have learned "in the trenches."

The Effective Schools Process is the first step to school reform, if you will. The Effective Schools Process complements new pedagogical strategies, such as cooperative learning, mastery learning, the Comer Process, Essential Schools (curriculum development, Re: Learning), Accelerated Schools, Comprehension and Cognition, and other curriculum initiatives. The two elements — the Effective Schools Process and the instructional program — are necessary to accomplish school reform.

The schools or district set their mission, goals, and objectives and then decide how to accomplish these goals and objectives through a strategic plan. Designing and agreeing on the strategic plan is part of the Effective Schools Process, which requires that the specific initiatives be prioritized, planned, implemented, evaluated, and refined in a cycle that repeats over two or three years.

Often, a school's interest in implementing a particular classroom method, such as cooperative learning, will set in motion the Effective Schools Process. Teachers who are trained in the procedures of cooperative learning see that they need to implement new scheduling (longer subject periods) and alternative (heterogeneous) grouping. Yet the district, teachers association, or state's school codes may have contrary policies. Thus the teachers begin to see the need for new communication channels and coordination and control mechanisms, which the Effective Schools Process can produce at school and district levels. And they recognize the need to secure waivers of policies and requirements at all levels.

Perhaps in setting up the new structures needed to implement cooperative learning (such as new assessment and reporting systems and data gathering and interpretation skills) the teachers, principals, and support staff realize that they need to meet, frequently at first, later only once a month. And in this realization they stumble onto the most perplexing barrier to school reform:

3

How do public school educators find (or make) enough time to make decisions and plan for change?

The discovery of the importance of time in the school setting is the secret of success of the Effective Schools Process. Schlechty (1990) has stated it well:

> In the elementary school the idea of periods is not so prominent as in high school, but state mandates regarding the number of minutes of instruction in certain subjects make elementary schools nearly as time-bound as high schools constrained by the Carnegie unit. The result is that teachers, faculties, and principals have — and, more important, feel that they have — little control over the way time is allocated in school. Furthermore, the one commodity that teachers and administrators say they do not have enough of, even more so than money, is time: time to teach, time to converse, time to think, time to plan, time to talk, even time to go to the restroom or to drink a cup of coffee. The time situation is so harried in schools that many teachers' unions have launched major campaigns to ensure that teachers are free from students for a lunch period of not less than twenty minutes. Time is indeed precious in school. (p. 73)

The Effective Schools Process *finds* time for change. Through staff development, specifically using the School-Based Instructional Leadership (SBIL) professional development modules created by the National Center for Effective Schools Research and Development (NCESRD), teachers, administrators, support staff, students, and parents can be taught the fundamental skills needed for bringing about real school reform. They also will be introduced to outstanding pedagogical programs and instructional initiatives. SBIL modules focus on:

- shared decision making
- school-based management
- strategic planning
- data collection for management information/instructional effectiveness
- team building

- conflict resolution
- consensus building
- gathering and interpreting student performance data
- setting standards and curriculum content topics
- deciding prerequisites, scope, and sequence of curriculum objectives
- setting essential teaching objectives
- comprehension and cognition program (National Urban Alliance)
- awareness of time on task, engaged time
- awareness of transition time
- dimensions of learning
- cooperative learning
- mastery learning
- interdisciplinary unit planning and assessment
- reporting student performance
- gathering, interpretation, and use of data on school reform indicators
- self-discipline, school discipline code enforcement

Developing these skills enables educators to use time effectively and thus to *find* time to create change.

What started out in the 1970s as a university-based inquiry into the nature of schools that taught all children the intended curriculum has spread through nearly two decades of demonstration projects to school reform efforts all over the United States.

Charles Teddlie and Samuel Stringfield recently published their 10-year longitudinal study on school effects in *Schools Make a Difference* (1993). Daniel Levine and Eugene Eubanks (1986, 1992) continue to assess and critique Effective Schools. But the Effective Schools Research and the development of the comprehensive Effective Schools Process have now been abandoned by almost all university research and development units. In contrast, the regional education laboratories — notably the Northwest Regional Laboratory, the Midcontinent Regional Laboratory, the North Central Regional Laboratory, and the Southwest Educational Development Laboratory — continue to develop and apply Effective Schools Research in the field by training practitioners and state departments of education.

This book examines Effective Schools as a reform philosophy, body of research, and process for today and the coming years. Chapter 1 begins with a thorough definition of this philosophy and the conceptual rationale that undergirds Effective Schools. Chapter 2 provides a succinct history of the Effective Schools movement,

Chapters 3, 4, and 5 examine specific aspects of the Effective Schools Process, beginning with the classroom, moving on to the culture of the entire school, and then looking specifically at curriculum development, student assessment, staff development, and accountability. In effect, these three chapters mirror the grassroots development process of Effective Schools, starting closest to the student and teacher interaction and then proceeding in bottom-up fashion to more global matters.

Chapter 6 profiles four school superintendents who have used the Effective Schools Research and the Effective Schools Process to transform their districts. The school systems portrayed are Spring Branch, Texas; St. John's County, Florida; Springfield, Massachusetts; and Glendale, Arizona.

Finally, in Chapter 7, we look into the future, examining the challenges that schools will face in the coming years and discussing how the Effective Schools philosophy can be applied to meet those challenges.

Chapter 1

Effective Schools Defined

We know what it takes to create a learning community. This is the same learning community (or learning organization) that has been successfully designed in American and international business. As we documented in *Making School Reform Happen* (1993) and *Keepers of the Dream* (1994), rich and poor districts alike have been transformed by the Effective Schools Process into creative, active learning communities. Not only do these districts continue to improve, but their progress has deepened and broadened. Teachers and staff in these schools have pursued school effectiveness as a constant adventure in the enhancement of knowledge for everyone in the school.

It is not important at this juncture whether the original impetus came "down" from administration or "up" from the classroom. What matters is that the learning community is the model of equitable, quality school reform.

In the learning community, an active mission and specific goals are accomplished by dynamic, collaborative means through shared decisions made at the school site. The moral imperative that all children learn is the guiding force of the Effective Schools Process. This requires a gradual, research-guided transformation of a school's shared beliefs in order to envision a new school culture. From these beliefs grow the correlates, or structural characteristics, of the Effective Schools Process. The process is comprehensive and systemic. Its success depends on everyone who is involved in the education enterprise being accountable. Thus personal fulfillment is a key to success.

Personal fulfillment is one of those "touchy-feely" notions that business leaders and, to a lesser degree, educators have been wary to embrace. It did not fit the image of the aggressive, goal-oriented, 1980s "doer." But in the 1990s the push is on "being" as much as "doing," thanks in some measure to such highly regarded books as *Stewardship* (1993) by Peter Block, in which he emphasizes the "successful integration of the spirit, the marketplace, and politics" (p. 227). The higher purposes in life now are not only discussed but pursued. Finally, some 25 years after Ron Edmonds first verbalized it, it has become fashionable to speak of the moral imperative that all children can learn — and must learn — the intended curriculum.

As recently as 1992, when we were completing research on *Making School Reform Happen*, teachers in Effective Schools spoke openly of all children learning; however, the voices in many other schools were silent about that belief. Now teachers and principals in schools throughout the country not only talk enthusiastically about all children learning, they cheer the ascendancy of that belief and fight to demonstrate the power of high expectations.

The passion of this shared vision is transforming as well as transcending. Peter Senge, in *The Fifth Discipline*, wrote:

> When people truly share a vision they are connected, bound together by a common aspiration. Personal visions derive their power from an individual's deep caring for the vision. Shared visions derive their power from a common caring. In fact, we have to believe that one of the reasons people seek to build shared visions is their desire to be connected in an important undertaking. Shared vision is vital for the learning organization because it provides the focus and energy for learning. (1990, p. 206)

Despite a cacophony of conservative rhetoric — recently reinforced by Charles Murray and Richard Herrnstein's political tome, *The Bell Curve* (1994) — there is a strong belief running deeply to the core of many schools that, indeed, all children *can* learn. A dedicated corps of professionals continues to prove each day in our public schools that the change process has been activated and the result is higher, more complete achievement for all students. Schools across America are proving that the negative, reactionary, doomsday rhetoric is wrong. Yes, there are problems; neglectful, abusive schools do exist. But there also are thousands of school districts that routinely attest to the power and lasting promise of a shared vision that all children can learn.

The Correlates

For the past quarter-century, this shared vision has been the basis of the Effective Schools correlates. In fact, we have reached the silver anniversary of those seven mini-commandments of education with which Ron Edmonds and John Frederickson started working in the early 1970s. There are some guiding values in life that do not and should not change.

The development of the Effective Schools Process has proceeded from the dynamic interactions of these correlates:

1. *A clearly stated and focused mission on learning for all.* The group (faculty, administration, parents) shares an understanding of and a commitment to the instructional goals, priorities, assessment procedures, and personal and group accountability. Their focus is always, unequivocally, on the student.
2. *A safe and orderly environment for learning.* The school provides a purposeful, equitable, businesslike atmosphere that encourages, supports, allows mistakes, and is free of fear. School is a place that does no harm to developing psyches and spirits.
3. *Uncompromising commitment to high expectations for all.* Those who are leaders empower others to become leaders who believe and demonstrate that all students can attain

mastery of essential skills. This commitment is shared by professionals who hold high expectations of themselves.

4. *Instructional leadership.* Although initially coming from a principal, teacher, or administrator, the goal is to include all participants as instructional leaders as their knowledge expands as a result of staff development. New insights excite and inspire. In the accountable learning community, everyone is a student and all can be leaders.

5. *Opportunity to learn is paramount.* Time is allocated for specific and free-choice tasks. The learning process is created by those closely involved with students, understanding that every child's learning process is unique and that every child's life experience is valuable to the learning process. Students take part in making decisions about goals and tasks.

6. *Frequent monitoring of progress.* Effective Schools evaluate the skills and achievements of all students and teachers. No intimidation is implied. Rather, monitoring often is individualized and long-term, with improvement in learning as the goal.

7. *Enhanced communication.* Efforts to improve and expand communication between home, school, and community extend the "learning community" beyond the classroom walls. The community at large, especially parents, is given the opportunity to become true partners in the learning process, not only as guides but as participants. Learning for all means, simply, *all*.

These Effective Schools correlates have become the framework of reform. They provide the organizational imperatives for pervasive school change, and they support ongoing renewal because they do not change. They are always there to reinforce a strategy or indicate an option. They are the means to the end. They buttress the shared purpose of learning for all in order to create not just knowledge workers, not just a skilled workforce, but a community of lifelong learners.

Teachers, individually and in collaboration with their colleagues, give the correlates their power and relevance. They put a face on the moral purpose of educational change.

In the January 1985 issue of the *Elementary School Journal*, Michael Fullan discussed the success of the Effective Schools Process that was then evident. He wrote of the success that comes from applying the correlates and understanding process variables, such as a guiding value system. In his latest book, *Change Forces: Probing the Depths of Educational Reform* (1993), Fullan discusses the vital role of a moral imperative in successful reform:

> Moral purpose and change agentry synergize care and competence, equity and excellence. . . . When teachers work on personal vision building and see how their commitment to making a difference in the classroom is connected to the wider purpose of education, it gives practical and moral meaning to their profession. When they pursue learning through constant inquiry, they are practicing what they preach, benefiting themselves and their students by always learning. . . . When one teacher collaborates with another, or many teachers work in a new alliance with each other and outside partners, they are enlarging their horizons as they lengthen and strengthen the levers of improvement. (p. 145)

The Process

The Effective Schools Process is a professional development process — based on the tenets of Effective Schools Research — that addresses the motivators and management of change in order to create organizational learning and organizational momentum for beneficial and lasting change. That process is designed:

- to develop skills and attitudes for shared leadership on school improvement teams;
- to synthesize, coordinate, and integrate otherwise fragmented efforts around a common framework that focuses on student learning;
- to build internal capacity for dissemination and follow-up;

11

- to provide a readiness base for more ambitious or extensive restructuring efforts; and
- to encourage collaboration among school improvement facilitators.

The Effective Schools Process also is systemic. School districts have built on and expanded this process over the years to foster improvement in organizational and management strategies as well as to provide a means — through the school improvement teams and staff development — for teachers to become comfortable with changing pedagogy. Ron Edmonds said:

> We teach people two different things: 1) We teach them the minimum school behaviors that they must obtain. 2) We, at least, introduce them to the range of teacher behaviors more consistently associated with diminished discipline problems, heightened achievement, and better organization. Then we go on to teach them a repertoire of designs for doing those things. We leave them to decide whether they will use one of those designs, or another one that they have thought of themselves.
>
> We teach that there are no instructional problems that have not already been solved. The only issue is, whether or not the organization makes available to principals and teachers the extraordinary repertoire of school behaviors and teacher behaviors that will produce mastery for the full range of the population. (NCESRD 1989, p. 7)

If politicians, boards, and school administrators are interested in a top-down approach to school change or a hard-and-fast recipe for school reform that guarantees success in a specific number of years, that is not the Effective Schools Process. This process is a multi-year, cyclical process with many potential entry points for school districts. The chosen entry point will depend on the school's culture or the district's present organization and what they perceive as institutional pluses, negatives, and barriers to change. For example, some schools will start by clarifying their mission, some with a realization that they need to make more effective use of data, and others from a desire to decentralize decisions.

Varied entry points allow for the Effective Schools Process to be ongoing — with concurrent, ongoing assessment by those involved. When one goal is achieved, another is established.

Similarly, the process is not concerned with a single, specific classroom method or pedagogy. It is about giving teachers the support and information they need in order to use methods of instruction that best meet each student's needs. Effective Schools is about knowledge, about creating mindful, thinking workers in the classroom, the central office, and the board room. It is a process that emphasizes collaboration, cooperation, and team-work with a strong preference for vertical teams composed of teachers, administrators, parents, community members, central office representatives, and students. This notion of vertical teams extends to all school stakeholders in the community. Thus the Effective Schools Process allows — indeed, encourages — good plans and strategies and their implementation to "bubble up" with support from the top. Adherents of this process believe that no school or district can effectively operate without a sufficient consensus among the stakeholders.

Collaboration and cooperation extend naturally to shared leadership principles. Edmonds spoke of the principles of shared leadership that have become the hub of today's school reform:

> If you want to modify an organization that in any way is remotely permanent, then you must share authority. Authority must be representative; that is, everybody involved in the system has a task — parents, teachers, administrators, aides, and support service people — are represented on the governing group. (NCESRD 1989, p. 44)

Means of implementation vary with districts because of their varied cultures, personalities, and developmental stages. But those schools and districts that stay focused on their mission and vision are most able to find viable means.

The Vision

The Effective Schools Process is designed to help schools stop failing to educate all their students. Philip Schlechty has worked closely with leaders involved in school reform, in particular in Jefferson County, Kentucky. In his 1990 book, *Schools for the 21st Century*, endorsed with an introduction by then-Governor Bill Clinton, Schlechty proposed that as America becomes more information- and technology-based, the individuals who have knowledge and know how to use it will have the power. He wrote:

> Indeed, the major democratic revolution that many reformers have looked for may come about precisely because the means of production in an information based society is based on knowledge and the ability to work to create, invent, and to solve problems. Those who have knowledge-work skills will have access to the levers of power and those who are denied knowledge will be denied access. . . .
>
> The knowledge-work metaphor, properly understood, insists on standards, for it is standards, rather than rules and procedures, that govern life among knowledge workers. Moreover, knowledge work demands extreme attention to elements of culture, for it is with cultural elements (ideas, propositions, beliefs, symbols, and modes of explanation) that knowledge workers work. (pp. 38, 42)

That culture of the learning organization is the model that business leaders began to expound in the early 1980s. Tom Peters (*In Search of Excellence*, 1982), Jim Kouzes and Barry Posner (*The Leadership Challenge*, 1987), Stephen Covey (*The 7 Habits of Highly Effective People*, 1989), and other authors wrote of the necessity of a culture of shared vision, where all workers are involved in a company's growth and in their own growth. Peter Senge, in *The Fifth Discipline* (1990), asserts that this culture of shared vision is defined in these ways:

1. People's capacity to create the results they desire is continually expanding.

2. New and expansive patterns of thinking are nurtured. Collective aspiration is set free.
3. People are continually learning how to learn together.

No great leap of faith is needed to move these tenets from the board room to a superintendent's office, a principal's office, a teachers' work room, and the classroom. This idea of the learning community has been, and continues to be, the essence of the Effective Schools Process.

It is a process that keeps its eye on the vision. While other programs have wavered in vision and scope, Effective Schools practitioners and researchers have stayed true to theirs. Schlechty sees that kind of commitment as the key to genuine, ongoing success:

> The key to restructuring our schools resides in a reformulation of purpose and the creation of a vision of schools that is consistent with that purpose. Regardless of the way the purpose is stated, the statement must be based on the bedrock belief that every child can learn and that every child will learn if he or she is presented with the right schoolwork to do. (1990, p. 62)

This recent talk of shared vision and reformulation of purpose serves to validate what many educators who have been working in the Effective Schools Process for a quarter of a century believe. When Effective Schools began, the idea that "all children can learn the intended curriculum" was viewed as merely liberal rhetoric. But over the years this "rhetoric" has grown into a cry for equity from urban, rural, and suburban schools and from rich and poor districts alike.

The Promise

In his 1990 book, *Teachers for Our Nation's Schools*, John Goodlad wrote of a "nation awakening" and spoke of the "pioneering research and robust, informed opinions of a black scholar named Ronald Edmonds." He noted Edmonds' findings that black children progressed in schools where teachers and staff believed in the students and in themselves. It was Edmonds and the Effective Schools findings, wrote Goodlad, that "inspired many principals to believe that they and teachers had an important role to play in improving the quality of their schools" (p. 5).

In order to understand the promise that lies in implementing Effective Schools, it is instructive to look again at the differences that Edmonds found some 25 years ago between high-achieving/improving schools and the low-achieving/declining schools. In the high-achieving/improving schools:

- Teachers believed that all their students could learn.
- Teachers had specific goals.
- Teachers were more task-oriented.
- Teachers were not satisfied with the status quo.
- Teachers had more supportive principals.
- The principal was a strong leader, supportive and visible.
- There was more monitoring of student achievement.
- Teachers had higher expectations for their students.
- Students were happier and worked harder.
- There was trust between students and faculty and administrators.

These differences seemed revolutionary to many educators in the late 1960s — especially when the effects of higher student achievement scores, fewer discipline problems, and more teacher and staff satisfaction were revealed. But these characteristics now are routinely viewed as the cornerstone of successful school reform. While the bad news may be that we are reaping the negative results of paying too little attention to these characteristics in some schools, the good news is that the idea of an accountable learning community has finally been broadly accepted in public education.

The truth is that if a child fails to learn, then schools must share the blame for that failure. Educators no longer can blame the student or his or her background with impunity. This does not deny that the odds are stacked against educators and the child. Poverty and disillusionment fed by new brands of racism; new, more subtle forms of discrimination; unemployment in minority communities; and other ills do not set the stage for positive life experiences, let alone positive school experiences. However, educators now are beginning to understand that their students' success depends, to a greater extent than previously believed, on the classroom climate, the pedagogy, and the school in general. Moreover their own fulfillment as professionals, as well as their own learning, is tied directly to the success of the students in their classrooms.

"It's real easy to teach a few children differently. You know, just pick out the kids you have decided in your mind will succeed and just teach them," said Judy Stevens during a personal interview with one of the authors in April 1993. Stevens is the executive director of Elementary Education for the Spring Branch, Texas, school system and one of this country's leading advocates of brain-compatible learning. "The real hard task is teaching all children equally," she said. "And equally means that we understand that each child's brain is valuable, but different. Each child is different, so we must teach them differently."

Teachers today, working within their learning communities, now can be armed with the latest scientific knowledge of how the brain works and how we learn. They have discovered that rote learning, lecture-oriented teaching, and irrelevant material belong to the schoolhouse of the past. Teaching, as we once knew it, failed many students because the essential pedagogy was flawed.

"Yes, finally we're saying that. Too late, too late, for too many," said Stevens. "But now we say it, many believe it, and finally, we are paying attention to the information the science and psychology departments have been trying to give us for years. Research, information, when applied in the classroom, proves beyond any doubt, that there is not a child — not one — out there who cannot learn the intended curriculum."

Building on an eight-year foundation of the Effective Schools Improvement Process, Stevens has brought into Spring Branch the latest research on multiple intelligences, brain-intuitive instruction, learning, interdisciplinary curriculum, and multi-dimensional assessment. Staff development is voluntary, but teachers in Spring Branch — and in districts across the country — are discovering that this knowledge opens the floodgates of learning for their students — and for themselves.

This knowledge about how children learn has been in the scientific community since the mid-1970s. So why are these insights just now breaking through the old guard? Many observers say that this revolution finally is happening because the docile, blond-haired, blue-eyed child who obeyed teacher commands, did the rote learning, and listened to the irrelevant lectures has been replaced by an often aggressive, often angry, darker-skinned child who presents a more demanding intellectual, moral, and emotional challenge to educators. These students bring the anger of the streets into the classroom. The failures rise, and it is difficult for schools to keep blaming the student. Finally, the schools must respond.

We believe the change will finally come because the success of the Effective Schools Process makes it imperative that we recognize the body of knowledge now available to reform the schools for the benefit of all students, teachers, and administrators.

Districts began working with the new pedagogy and the Effective Schools Process in the early 1980s. One such location was an inner-city subdistrict in St. Louis. Schools there were dumping grounds for some of the city's most troubled, "uneducable" children. The Effective Schools Process was implemented and, within three years, standardized test scores climbed beyond state and national averages, dropout rates and absenteeism plummeted, and teacher and staff morale soared. Parents cheered and community leaders became more involved in the schools than ever before.

Educators from across America and around the world (including Japan) trudged cautiously into the poverty-ravaged St. Louis slum to look at these schools. They left saying, "If it can happen there, it can happen anywhere." And it began to happen: in the farm lands of Kansas; in the growing Pacific Islander immigrant communities of Seattle; in San Diego; Milwaukee, Wisconsin; Glendale, Arizona; St. John's County, Florida; Prince Georges County and Frederick County, Maryland; Norfolk, Virginia; across South Carolina, Kentucky, Spanish Harlem, upstate New York; across the state of Connecticut and up into Vermont. The statistics of success began to accumulate, providing the data that proved the power of this process to ignite and renew districts.

An example of how far the rhetoric, and schools, have come can be seen in Springfield, Massachusetts, where Superintendent Peter Negroni spoke the words in 1993 that would have been heresy 10 years earlier:

> This is the first time in the history of public education that we are expected to educate all children equally. Heretofore the role of the American public school was chiefly to sort and select, to decide who would go to college and who would enter the world of work. Today, the new requirement of the school is to provide an effective and appropriate education for all children, no matter how they come to school. Our new vision that all children be successful has caught the public schools of America by surprise. This shift of responsibility to the school requires a critical shift in perspective. (Negroni 1993, p. 151)

The "new requirement" — at least it's being said. But it has not been a new requirement to those who have had the desire and the will to motivate change *within* the public schools. It comes as no new requirement to the teachers who understood John Dewey, often referred to as the father of educational philosophy, when he wrote about the need for learning to be a "unity of knowledge," involving real-life activities and relevant materials in the classroom. Dewey was advocating the so-called new pedagogy before the scientific community created the terminology. Today, 90 years later, it is called authentic learning (among other things); and across the country, teachers are discovering and tapping its power.

The Effective Schools Process embodies three distinct forces. First is insistence that all schools be places of learning for all.

Second is acceptance of the knowledge worker/learning organization as essential to the school reform process. These are the tenets sets forth by such practitioners as Peter Drucker (*Frontiers of Management*, 1987; *The Age of Discontinuity: Guidelines to Our Changing Society*, 1969), Peter Senge (*The Fifth Discipline*, 1990), Kouzes and Posner (*The Leadership Challenge*, 1987; *Credibility: How Leaders Gain and Lose It, Why People Demand It*, 1993), and organizational researchers Henry Levin (*Cost-Effectiveness of Four Educational Interventions*, 1984), James March (*Organizations*, 1958), and James Thompson (*Organizations in Action*, 1967).

Third is acceptance that unlearning old methods and learning new ones is essential to success. The doors of research have swung open, and new data and insights into how children learn are pouring out daily. Effective teachers are grabbing this new knowledge and running with it.

What worked in the past is not viable today, as emphasized by Fullan:

> Today the teacher who works for or allows the status quo is a traitor. Purposeful change is the new norm in teaching. It has been bouncing around within teaching for the past thirty years. It is time we realized that teachers above all are moral change agents in society — a role that must be pursued explicitly and aggressively. (1993, p.15)

Kouzes and Posner state that this realization, however treacherous it seems to be initially, is essential for true renewal:

> Leaders and constituencies must first acknowledge that what once worked no longer does, and then they must be able to enter into a zone of uncertainty that is at first frightening but from which they emerge energized and renewed. And unless people, organizations, and communities are renewed, they are overtaken by the chaos of decline and decay. (1993, p. 271)

That renewal is the promise of the Effective Schools Process.

Effective Schools and Total Quality

Recent interest in total quality management (TQM) is seren-dipitous, because Effective Schools is fully compatible with the principles set forth by W. Edwards Deming. In *Total Quality Education* (1993) Michael Schmoker and Richard Wilson praise TQM for its "adaptability, its capacity to embrace and refine much of what already is working." TQM is seen as a "template" that can be applied to various improvement endeavors. These authors specifically mention Effective Schools.

Educators involved in day-to-day school improvement see a strength of TQM in its smooth linkage with the correlates of Effective Schools. Both TQM and Effective Schools regard high expectations as a linchpin. Deming believed that any worker can do higher quality work if he or she is given training and opportunity. He believed that if the quality of the work for the bottom 25% of workers were accelerated, then the entire system would progress.

System is an essential concept in TQM and Effective Schools. Deming did not see the world, its institutions, or its people as sep-arate entities, each vying for a piece of turf. Rather, he believed in the entire world as a system and maintained that the failure to accept and act on that reality would have dangerous consequences.

Deming described four elements of profound knowledge as 1) appreciation for a system, 2) knowledge about variation, 3) theory of knowledge, and 4) psychology. These four elements intertwine with Effective Schools principles. Effective Schools requires that all people in the learning organization make a commitment and that the commitment become a way of life and not just a means of daily operation. Effective Schools requires the retraining of teachers, staff, and administrators in an understanding of the change they are creating. And the Effective Schools Process immerses the intellect and the spirit in learning.

The "process" part of the Effective Schools Process sets Effective Schools apart from other reform efforts. That process, profiled in this book, builds on changes in the roles of education practitioners. But the process also depends on the real change to come from the learning community itself or, as Deming would say, the system.

TQM and Effective Schools mesh together and build on each other. Their alignment is best depicted by an examination of Deming's 14 principles, as analyzed for educational impact by Schmoker and Wilson, and the Effective Schools Process:

1. *Create constancy of purpose toward improvement of product and service.* Teaching all students is the driving force of Effective Schools. Mission, focus, and goals are the foundation. Effective Schools is outcomes-based: All students can learn and succeed given the appropriate time and coaching. Academic outcomes must be specified and students are expected to perform to those standards.

2. *Adopt the new philosophy.* Strong instructional leadership, reinforced by retraining that affects teachers and staff as much as administrators, is a correlate. Effective Schools and Total Quality Management agree in a belief that people can accomplish what is needed if given the information, tools, and training necessary for success.

3. *Cease dependence on mass inspection.* Deming advocates "managing employees in ways that encourage them to monitor and inspect their own work." Effective Schools, through more individualized monitoring processes and teachers' reliance more on performance and authentic assessment, infuses schools with self-directed learning and grading that push students beyond mediocrity and complacency.

4. *End the practice of awarding business on the basis of price tag alone.* Quality of the work — the depth of the students' learning — is a key component of Effective Schools, and multiple measures of effectiveness are essential.

5. *Improve constantly and forever the system of production and service.* Effective Schools Research emphasizes that improvement is ongoing. It does not happen overnight, and it is never finished. A school that is not improving is declining.

6. *Institute training.* The rallying cry for Effective Schools reform is training and retraining.
7. *Institute leadership.* For Deming, leadership was creating a workplace that allowed people to do their best quality work. Effective Schools insists on an involved "teaching" leader, a leader who mingles easily and happily with staff and who becomes involved with every aspect of the learning community.
8. *Drive out fear.* Schools often view "reform" as criticism of the work they are doing. They do not understand that change is designed to help. The Effective Schools Process recognizes that no one can grow in a threatened professional environment. Instead of fear, a learning community is built on trust between student and teacher, teacher and principal, and teacher and parent. In an atmosphere of trust, people dare to take risks.
9. *Break down barriers between staff areas.* To create a genuine learning community, there cannot be a division of ranks. Everyone must work together for the stated purpose of the community. Effective Schools strives for equity and collegiality within the ranks. The improvement of student achievement depends on collaboration.
10. *Eliminate slogans, exhortations, and targets for the workforce.* On the surface, this seems antithetical to Effective Schools. However, while targets and slogans often mark the beginnings of reform, the emphasis is on individual exhortations and targets that are set within the school. Mandates from on high are ineffective.
11. *Eliminate numerical quotas or targets for the workforce.* Data is collected as it is in any business, but academic goals and standards are established from the bottom up.
12. *Remove barriers to pride of workmanship.* Effective Schools practitioners "celebrate" the student and the learning community.

13. *Encourage education and self-improvement for everyone.* Professional and personal growth is expanded throughout the learning community.
14. *The transformation is everybody's job.* In an active, effective, performance-based school, the custodial staff and bus drivers also will be involved in the change process that brings them into the learning community.

TQM concepts are vital to the creation of a learning community in the Effective Schools sense. It is that learning community that is the promise of public education. It is the home of the means for accomplishing specific, enduring goals in fulfillment of the mission of teaching for learning for all.

Learning to Ride a Unicycle

William Raspberry, the Pulitzer Prize-winning columnist for the *Washington Post*, writing in August 1993 as children prepared to return to school after their summer break, admitted that even he, who believes that all children can learn, is "astonished when some unlikely children actually do" (1993, p. 17). He wrote about different learning communities, about Marva Collins in Chicago, Jaime Escalante in East Los Angeles, the kids at Franklin High in Philadelphia, and finally, about a report that described how every last child in a small-town school in Ohio learned how to ride a unicycle.

This book does not report stories of kids riding unicycles. It does document that teachers and students are doing extraordinary work. It documents the power of a new teaching and learning pedagogy, the return of hope, and the renewal of public schools across this nation through the empowerment of learning communities. It is about a shared vision and the power of high expectations. It is about a process that transforms and transcends. And it all begins with a small but mighty belief that all children can learn. As Raspberry comments:

It's probably too much to ask — even most ministers seem reluctant to ask their congregations to live as though they believe the faith they profess. But wouldn't it be nice if all of us — teachers, parents, politicians, business leaders, journalists — would pledge just for the next semester to act as though we really do believe all our children can learn?

It just might mark the beginning of an academic revival, a reaffirmation of the faith we all confess and the literal salvation of our nation. (p. 17)

Chapter 2

Development of the Effective Schools Process

The history of the Effective Schools "movement" is remarkable. At times, the movement has surged like a tidal wave. At other times, it has seemed little more than an eddy.

One of the reasons for this inconsistency is that none of the early researchers of Effective Schools in the 1960s and 1970s was aware of the vast literature on organizational behavior that was then available. As social psychologists and sociologists, they used sources from sociology, political science, and psychology. These sources did not contain the extensive findings from management studies of organizational behavior, specifically the management of change. Thus the early researchers failed to take into account the necessity of considering organizational development before the schools began their change or development efforts. Consequently, the educators who attempted to apply the early Effective Schools Research often were flying on faith.

Some inconsistency also arose because Effective Schools is a process model. Over the years the Effective Schools movement has borrowed from numerous disciplines: psychology, sociology, education administration, organizational behavior studies, curriculum and instruction, and political science, especially the policy implementation literature. While research in the field of education always has been multidisciplinary to some extent, most investigations even today tend to focus on a single area, such as administration or educational psychology. The diverse, wide-angle focus of the Effective Schools Research left many observers initially confused or skeptical.

But let us start at the beginning.

Roots of Effective Schools Research

Wilbur Brookover stated that the first inquiries that were to become known as Effective Schools Research began with a genial conversation between colleagues one morning in the College of Education at Michigan State University. The professors were most interested in the then-current work of George Weber of the Council on Basic Education (1971). Weber had studied four urban "exemplary" elementary schools and suggested eight characteristics that influenced the reading achievement of students.

Weber's findings reflected the early work that Brookover and his colleagues had carried out in the late 1950s and early 1960s on student self-concept of ability and school achievement. Brookover was particularly interested in the study of school "climate" (which he defined as the school social system, or manifestation of school culture) and the effect of school climate on student self-concept and achievement.

Earlier, Brookover (1959) had studied the relationship of student self-concept to classroom learning and academic grades. He also studied the relationship of student self-concept of academic ability — or the individual's perceived expectations of significant others — to student achievement. "Self-concept" in these early studies was described as "the individual's assessment of his or her ability to learn in the school context" (Brookover, Paterson, and Thomas 1962). Self-concept changes over time, depending on the interactions of the student with significant others and their evaluations of the student at home and in school.

Brookover also studied the relationships of patterns of differentiation (grouping, tracking) among elementary and secondary school students, and these students' self-concepts. Brookover's interest in studying the effects of the broader school social organization on classroom learning emerged from these studies.

In 1973, Brookover, Richard Gigliotti, Ronald Henderson, and Jeffrey Schneider carried out a major study that described three student factors and three teacher factors that accounted for most of the differences in student achievement in high-achieving and low-achieving schools with similar student compositions:

> The first of these is the factor which we call the student's sense of futility. This includes the student's sense of control within the school's social environment and his perception of whether or not the teachers care or are committed to his achievement. The two expectation-evaluation-self-concept factors, one oriented toward the present situation and the other the future, also account for a considerable proportion of the variance in achievement. The parallel factors in the teacher complex also account for some of the differences. The students' sense of futility, the teachers' belief in the improvability of the student and the two sets of present and future expectations and evaluation factors consistently distinguish between the high and low achievement schools. The teacher's belief in the improvability is particularly relevant in black schools. The school climates of black schools are distinguished from the white schools by sense of control and the level of expectations and evaluations.

In 1973, Ronald Edmonds, an assistant superintendent in the Department of Public Instruction of Michigan and a former colleague of Brookover's, had just left that department to join the faculty at the Harvard School of Education. He became the director of the Center for Urban Studies there, and soon after arriving joined with John Frederickson to begin the research project, "Search for Effective Schools: The Identification and Analysis of City Schools that Are Instructionally Effective for Poor Children." This project was funded by the Carnegie Corporation of New York.

At the same time, Brookover and Lawrence Lezotte were using student test data (standardized, criterion-referenced tests given in grades 4 and 7) from the Michigan State Department of Education to identify elementary schools characterized by consistent pupil performance improvement or decline. Brookover and Lezotte (1977) reported 10 descriptors that differentiated improving schools from declining schools. (They compared eight schools in all.) Using these findings and other similar findings in 20 elementary schools in the Detroit Model Cities Neighborhood, Edmonds and Frederickson (1978) then asked the question, "Are there schools that are instructionally effective for poor children?" "Instructionally effective" was defined as being at or above the city average in norms for standardized testing. "Instructionally ineffective" was defined as being below the city average. Using these criteria, they found that eight of the 20 schools were effective in teaching math, nine were judged to be effective in teaching reading, and five were judged to be effective in teaching both math and reading.

Desiring a larger sample size, Edmonds and Frederickson moved on to analyzing data from the Equal Educational Opportunity Survey — or EEOS (Coleman et al. 1966) — that had been gathered from the northeast quadrant of the country. From there they went on to Lansing, Michigan, to conduct an on-site study of all pupils in grades 3 through 7. They then returned to Detroit to gather similar data for pupils in elementary grades in schools whose pupil population was at least 15% low-income.

From this expanded study, reported in 1979, came the original effective schools correlates, "the most tangible and indispensable characteristics of effective schools." As Edmonds put it:

> They have strong administrative leadership without which the disparate elements of good schooling can be neither brought together nor kept together. Schools that are instructionally effective for poor children have a climate of expectation in which no children are permitted to fall below minimum but efficacious levels of achievement. The school's atmosphere is orderly without being rigid, quiet without being oppressive, and generally conducive to the instructional business at hand. Effective schools get that way partly by

making it clear that pupil acquisition of basic school skills takes precedence over all other school activities. When necessary, school energy and resources can be diverted from other business in furtherance of the fundamental objectives. The final effective school characteristic to be set down is that there must be some means by which pupil progress can be frequently monitored. These means may be as traditional as classroom testing on the day's lesson or as advanced as criterion referenced system-wide standardized measures. The point is that some means must exist in the school by which the principal and the teachers remain constantly aware of pupil progress in relationship to instructional objectives. (1979, p. 22)

Sticking to the Goal

The goal of teaching all children the intended curriculum involved systemic reform from the beginning. By 1982, Edmonds realized that even though the unit of change was the school, the entire district had to reorganize, to alter key roles, and to define more carefully its stakeholders' responsibilities. A basic tenet of organization behavior is that "you cannot change just one thing." In open systems, such as schools and school districts, unless systemic change is created and monitored, the organization will simply adapt to external pressures, rather than changing to meet the stated mission (Katz and Kahn 1966, pp. 2-4).

Also, organizational restructuring, even when carried out according to theory and with correct and pervasive implementation, does not ensure success. The will and commitment to achieve a mission, goals, and objectives; to acquire new organizational learning; and to develop a new school and district culture must be present (Brookover and Erickson 1969; Duncan and Weiss 1979; Taylor 1984).

After Brookover and his colleagues studied school climate, they realized that a good school climate, which is the manifestation of the school culture, is crucial to successful teaching and learning. Slowly, over the decade of the 1970s, the characteristics of unusually effective schools emerged. Studies by George Weber (1971), Brookover and colleagues (1977, 1979), Edmonds and Frederickson (1978), Gilbert Austin (1979), Phi Delta Kappa (1980), Tomlinson (1980), James Comer (1980), and in Great Britain, by Michael Rutter and colleagues (1979), all came to similar conclusions.

The characteristics of Effective Schools, referred to as "the correlates," were never intended as a prescription, recipe, or checklist. The correlates are characteristics that seem to be associated with higher student achievement and other indicators of school and student success. These correlates, at various times ranging in number from 6 to 11 (or more in some districts and states, a fact that bedevils basic researchers) are organizational variables that help school people diagnose the strengths and weaknesses of a school. The Connecticut Questionnaire, designed by Shoemaker and Villanova in 1983, is a good example of this organizational diagnosis procedure.

The Effective Schools correlates are fundamental to understanding the dynamics of organization change that occur when the belief that all children can learn the intended curriculum meshes with the restructuring of roles, responsibilities, rules, and reports. The Effective Schools Process, which evolved as a model for school improvement from the application of Effective Schools Research in the early and mid-1980s in the United States and Great Britain, is built on these fundamentals. The correlates must be in place in a school before real school reform can be effected.

In truth the correlates turn out to be those variables in the organization that can be manipulated to foster organizational momentum for change. When orchestrated by the school principal, the faculty, or the school council, the correlates supply the energy and strategic processes to carry out and sustain organization change. Indeed, these often-slighted descriptors of Effective Schools are powerful organizational forces for school and district reform when they are applied with competence and commitment (Taylor 1984; Fullan 1991).

Thus the inquiry that began as a research study to describe the culture or learning climate of schools that were effective now has developed into a process model whereby practitioners can be trained to develop their own Effective Schools. The correlates, refined through more than a decade of application, represent those characteristics and processes that make the difference between schools that are effective and those that are not.

Refining the Model

When one of the fundamental correlates is left out, the school climate is *not* radically changed, and so an Effective School does not result. The presence of the correlates alone cannot ensure school effectiveness, but it makes success more probable. Thus much of the development of Effective Schools during the decade of the 1980s centered on refining and standardizing the process model of Effective Schools.

The most persistent criticism of the Effective Schools Research (for example, Purkey and Smith 1983) is that Effective Schools means many things to many people. We have argued that in applied research such "inconsistency" of implementation is not unusual, given the varied circumstances — political, social, economic, and experiential — found in each school district. Indeed, researchers often learn a great deal about the political, social, and economic contexts of school reform in a given district by studying the correlates that are addressed and those that are omitted.

For example, in the early 1980s schools often would pick and choose which of the Effective Schools correlates they would implement. While the research called for all of the fundamental (or primary) correlates to be implemented in order to create the structural readiness for change, the schools' political climates often did not favor such strategies as the disaggregation of data or the frequent monitoring of student performance. Where student monitoring was done at all, it usually was done with standardized, norm-referenced achievement tests, administered twice a year. This procedure for student performance assessment did not meet Brookover's and Edmonds' criterion for "frequent school monitoring." But it was the only form of assessment for schools at that time that satisfied both the political requirements of the so-called excellence movement (then at its zenith of influence) and the demands of "equal opportunity" and "comparability of programs."

Reality tends to waylay theory. In the decade of the 1980s, the excellence movement grew in influence; and "equity in excellence," proposed by Effective Schools practitioners and school effectiveness researchers, often was disregarded or considered to be merely a university pipe dream, as school people attempted to respond to the political realities of the Reagan and Bush Administrations' views on school reform and restructuring.

After the death of Edmonds in 1983, the Effective Schools movement slowed and little by little became fragmented. For example, William Spady took the "frequent monitoring" and "shared mission" correlates and emphasized the measurement of student outcomes, building on Mastery Learning. The results-orientation that originated with Effective Schools, Mastery Learning, and school effectiveness research was refined and became Outcome-Based Education (OBE). But OBE neglected the need for cultural change, human relations, and interactive communication strategies. Recently Spady has expanded his program and added the word "transformational" to depict a more comprehensive model that deals with cultural change. But some educators find that OBE is very "top-down" in design and decision making.

Other consultants, both independent and university-based, became experts in one or two of the correlates. Sometimes, they added a few of the other correlates in order "to get school improvement going." By picking and choosing to suit their own agendas, they ended up confusing many schools and districts about what the Effective Schools Research really said.

For a while, the university researchers who had lead the movement — Matthew Miles, Charles Teddlie, Richard Andrews, David Dwyer, David Clark, Rufus Young, Bruce Joyce, Dale

Mann, Stephen Miller, Maureen McCormick-Larsen, Joseph Murphy, Sam Stringfield, Philip Hallinger, and Karen Seashore-Louis, as well as Lezotte, Brookover, and colleagues at Michigan State — continued to investigate the role of the correlates in school reform. By 1984, most of these researchers were in schools, actually doing action research with many of the practitioners and stakeholders in districts around the country. Such books as *Innovation Up Close* (Huberman and Miles 1984) led to innovations in research design that emphasized new ways of collecting and interpreting qualitative data.

Also in the early 1980s, most regional education laboratories continued to train practitioners in "the correlates" and the beginning stages of the Effective Schools Process. Each lab developed its own version. However, because the labs saw the importance of keeping the model largely intact, most of what was known from Effective Schools Research until 1986 was incorporated. This research was school-based; research on school district's roles and responsibilities in change had yet to be incorporated. However, an assessment instrument, The Connecticut Questionnaire, was developed by Joan Shoemaker and Robert Villanova (1983), so that school-site needs assessment using the correlates as catagories was possible.

In 1986, the National Council on Effective Schools was disbanded, and the National Center for Effective Schools Research and Development (NCESRD) was planned. In 1987, following approval by Michigan State University, funding was obtained from a private foundation, and the NCESRD was established in the MSU School of Education.

In the years from 1987 to 1989, the NCESRD focused school change around the correlates of Effective Schools and the research that proceeded from the seminal writings of Effective Schools researchers. Also, many organization behavior theories from management literature were added to the research repertoire of Effective Schools. The Cadre of Fellows of NCESRD — a group of 70 principals, superintendents, state education department leaders, university researchers, and central office research and evaluation, and curriculum and instruction specialists — kept the Effective Schools model before states, districts, and individual schools. This cadre, led by Larry Lezotte and Lydia McCue, included the primary consultants who would help educators implement school change and school reform using the still-evolving Effective Schools model.

The Hawkins-Stafford Act, passed in April 1988, was the first comprehensive federal legislative attempt to promote school reform. It described the best currently available programs and processes and declared that public monies from Chapter 1 and Chapter 2 could be used for school improvement. Foremost among these programs was Effective Schools. Specifically, the planning process recommended in Effective Schools Research was declared one of the most successful processes for school improvement. This was the first time that Effective Schools was made an explicit option that districts could fund with federal money. The downside to this legislation was that, as often as not, anything specified in the bill could be waived at the state level.

By 1989, the federal General Accounting Office (GAO) estimated, in its report to Representative Augustus F. Hawkins (*Effective Schools Programs: Their Extent and Characteristics* 1989), that more than 6,500 school districts used "effective schools programs" of some type. However, only about 2,000 of these districts disaggregated student outcome data, an essential component of the Effective Schools model. Where there is no disaggregation of measured outcomes, the improvement effort amounts to little more than a shell game. Standards are set low — still true for many state minimum-mastery tests — and 80% or 90% of students meet those standards. The faster students pull up the average, and the slower students are neglected — or worse, they are not expected to do better.

For the leaders in the Effective Schools movement, the legislation was significant. But much remained to be done. A major factor in the development of Effective Schools was the relocation of NCESRD to University of Wisconsin-Madison in 1989.

NCESRD Moves to Wisconsin

Three researchers — Lawrence Lezotte, Barbara Taylor, and Beverly Bancroft — had taken the ideas of many prominent, active Effective Schools practitioners, researchers, and consultants and founded the National Center for Effective Schools Research and Development (NCESRD) at Michigan State University. Funded by a private foundation, the center set up shop in the Educational Administration Department of the College of Education, chaired by Philip Cusick. However, in spite of Cusick's interest in the center, he was not able to promote a harmonious relationship between Judith Lanier, dean of the College of Education at Michigan State University, and the director of the center, Larry Lezotte. Consequently, soon after its founding, the center moved to freestanding status in Okemos, Michigan.

This move proved fortuitous because the center's leadership was thus able to structure the center independent of the university's bureaucracy and academic willfulness. However, it quickly became apparent that the resources of a major research university were needed to protect, sustain, and nourish the fledgling NCESRD. Three universities were interested: the Peabody School at Vanderbilt University; the School of Education at the University of Texas in Austin; and the University of Wisconsin-Madison.

The University of Wisconsin-Madison held several advantages for the NCESRD. First, Andrew C. Porter, formerly of Michigan State and a colleague of Brookover and Lezotte, headed the Wisconsin Center for Education Research (WCER), where NCESRD would be housed. WCER, the largest education research facility in the world, was established in 1964, having been one of 12 national education research and development centers funded by the federal Office of Education. The research emerging from WCER, its outreach program in multicultural education, and its stable of nationally known policy centers complemented the NCESRD.

Second, because of this affiliation, NCESRD would be able to go directly to potential funders, subject only to Porter's authorization, rather than be required to submit proposals with specific authority from departments of the School of Education. Certain other advantages were negotiated in the affiliation agreement between the University of Wisconsin and NCESRD to make the center as independent as possible without being declared an "adjunct" organization, a status that it had initially demanded from WCER but that Porter said could not be granted. On 8 September 1989, NCESRD began operations in Wisconsin under the direction of Kent Peterson.

The reason for explaining these procedures and agreements is to provide some background about university-school district partnerships. The mission of a university, especially with regard to procuring research grants, is completely different from the mission of a school district. Therefore, many university-school partnerships are short-lived, even when their activities fall short of comprehensive school reform. Universities procure research grants to study interesting research questions; to pay the costs of research faculty, labs, and overhead; and to disseminate findings. In contrast, school districts procure research and development grants for pragmatic purposes: to improve curriculum design or practices in instruction, to design and implement a new program, to restructure the administrative relationships, to train faculty and administration, and so on.

NCESRD and WCER were interested in encouraging the type of applied research more typical of the schools and in training practitioners in the comprehensive Effective Schools Process. Thus, on 8 September 1989, NCESRD signed papers that affiliated the center with WCER. The center had three goals: 1) to achieve visibility for the center; 2) to obtain funds for an expanded organization to serve the increasing demand for professional development and consulting services to staff at the state offices of education, school districts, and some of the regional laboratories; and 3) to create the professional development modules based on Effective Schools Research and recent applied action research in the field.

The third goal was completed to a large extent by the summer of 1991. The basic philosophy and pragmatic framework of Effective Schools staff development had been written by 30 members of the Cadre of Fellows, under the leadership of Lydia McCue, in January 1989. Edie L. Holcomb, associate director for training and technical assistance at NCESRD, took the work of the cadre and almost single-handedly created a set of 10 professional development modules in 18 months. During 1991 and 1992 the modules were tested, evaluated, and refined; and the first Institutes for School-Based Instructional Leadership (SBIL), based on the modules, were held in June and July 1992 for school teams, facilitators, and trainers. By January 1993, the modules were ready for broad dissemination.

This brief historical summary sets the stage for our examination of how the Effective Schools Process works. Chapter 3 addresses the changing roles of teachers and administrators. Chapter 4 discusses how a school's culture is changed during the Effective Schools Process.

Chapter 3

Changing the Classroom

Where it has been implemented, the Effective Schools Process is changing how superintendents and central office administrators operate. It is increasing the accountability of school boards, revitalizing the leadership of principals, and encouraging greater involvement of parents and business.

But the most profound effect is in the classroom, where reform is given a face and moves beyond the buzzwords. Teachers are working more efficiently and more innovatively than ever before. They are changing children's lives. In order to do this, teachers have had to turn learning in the classroom on its head, shake it up, save some of the good pieces, toss out all the rest, take a deep breath, and build courageously.

"There's no question that it takes a lot of guts to teach effectively in the schools today," insists Judy Stevens, executive director of elementary education in Spring Branch, Texas. "Guts to question centuries of teacher indoctrination. Guts to be actively — ACTIVELY — involved in the child's learning process . . . and take ownership for the child's success or failure. It's not just a matter of accountability. It's ownership in that child. And it's a rejection of the punitive classroom."

Reasons for Change

Judy Stevens is not the first person to talk about what many believe is a damning legacy of the punitive, restrictive, and irrelevant classroom. In the 1890s, educator and philosopher John Dewey spoke of the need to teach children, not content, and to allow children to grow naturally and be inquisitive. In an address before a meeting of the American Psychological Association in 1899, Dewey said:

> The child is primarily one whose calling is growth. He is concerned with arriving at specific ends and purposes — instead of having a general framework already developed. He is engaged in forming habits rather than in definitely utilizing those already formed. (Dewey 1963, p. 297)

Dewey maintained that teachers took away a child's power over his own learning and, therefore, over the child's thinking process. He believed that teachers saw children as empty vessels to be filled with facts and figures determined by teachers. As Dewey pointed out in that 1899 speech:

> [W]e [teachers] provide next to no opportunities for the evolution of problems out of immediate experience, and allow next to no free mental play for selecting, assorting and adapting the experiences and ideas that make for their solution. (p. 299)

This standard still is maintained in the majority of schools and colleges. In the last decade, public schools have initiated broad reforms at the organization level, but the essential interactions between teacher and student have been neglected. Educators remain hesitant to take on the status quo of classroom teaching in spite of studies by Dewey, Brookover, John Goodlad, Seymour Sarason and William Glasser, and others that show that instructional techniques must change if schools are to be effective for all students.

Such change is difficult because it means changes in higher education and how teachers are trained to teach. It means that teachers in the field also must change in order to teach in new and unaccustomed ways. In fact, the entire education climate must be transformed, a realization discussed by Wilbur Brookover, who worked with Edmonds on much of the original Effective Schools Research. In a 1983 book, Brookover wrote:

> More recently my colleagues and I have expanded somewhat our usage of the concept of climate. To distinguish it from other aspects or conceptions of school climate, we have identified it as the school learning climate and define it as "the norms, beliefs, and attitudes reflected in institutional patterns and behavioral practices that enhance or impede student achievement" (Lezotte et al., 1980, p. 4). Thus the school learning climate includes not only the normative or ideological characteristics that we have previously emphasized but the school organizational characteristics and the instructional practices associated with student achievement outcomes.

John Goodlad (1984) in his well-known study, *A Place Called School*, wrote:

> What the schools in our sample did not appear to be doing in these subjects [English language arts, mathematics] was developing all those qualities commonly listed under "intellectual development": the ability to think rationally, the ability to use, evaluate, and accumulate knowledge, a desire for further learning. Only rarely did we find evidence to suggest instruction likely to go much beyond mere possession of information to a level of understanding its implications and either applying it or exploring its possible applications. Nor did we see activities likely to arouse students' curiosity or to involve them in seeking solutions to problems not already laid bare by teacher or textbook. (p. 236)

In later publications, Goodlad maintained that the major culprits in this crisis were the schools of education, an education system that did not encourage reflection, and a teacher corps too often socialized not to question tradition and to settle easily, complacently into mediocrity. In his 1994 book, *Educational Renewal: Better Teachers, Better Schools*, Goodlad noted that research now exists that reinforces the need to make fundamental changes in instructional techniques. But he doubts if such changes will occur:

> There is now a voluminous body of relevant literature, some of it organized in encyclopedic fashion, on human development, brain functioning, learning, teaching, and even directly on what beginning teachers should know. One would expect there to be a productive tension between the production and use of this knowledge, but the connection is exceedingly loose. It will be many years, if ever, before there are taxonomies that connect this knowledge base with the diverse, complex requirements of teaching in schools. (pp. 19-20)

We disagree. The productive tension that Goodlad addresses is the force behind the revolutionary changes now taking place in Effective Schools classrooms. Spring Branch, Texas, is a good example.

In the late 1980s, the 28,000-pupil school district changed from having some of the finest public schools in America to having some of the worst. That disastrous downhill slide was changed when the district leaders tossed out the status quo and began reforming and restructuring with the Effective Schools Process.

The changes of the 1980s in this district near Houston were, in a microcosm, the same changes that many districts experienced. Population shifts, the erosion of the tax base coupled with inflation, and increasing demands for new programs and more paperwork put the district at risk of failing to adequately educate many of its students. Implementing the Effective Schools Process has stopped the decline of this once-fine school district, and changes now are being made that are resulting in substantial improvements.

The changes in classrooms are among the most dramatic, innovative, and productive. Student test scores and grassroots research show that student achievement has increased. Students and teachers have regained confidence and enthusiasm for their work. According to Spring Branch educators, the Effective Schools Process has created not only the atmosphere for organization development and teaching reform, but the impetus and support for instructional innovation.

A strong foundation for these changes was agreement among teachers and administrators that the teachers first had to understand Effective Schools Research. They had to be involved in the improvement process within their school before taking steps toward reordering priorities in the classroom. Feeling empowered to make change decisions, led by competent principals and supported by the district's administration, teachers could accept the power of high expectations — both for themselves and for their students.

"If you feel it in your gut, really feel it, you're willing to take risks for what you feel," says Judy Stevens, head of Elementary Education. "With Effective Schools and the training the teachers and principals received, they knew in their guts their kids could do the work. These teachers knew they weren't reaching them by using the old ways. We set out to change that. The Effective Schools Process, with its emphasis on the moral imperative and the instructional leader, became the means to our end of improving every classroom for every child."

The Power of Moral Imperative

The idea of a moral imperative is important to school change. Absence of moral imperative has fostered schools riddled with failure. When John Goodlad wrote *Teachers for Our Nation's Schools* in 1990, he interviewed thousands of teachers and prospective teachers and found that "the idea of moral imperatives for teachers was virtually foreign in concept and strange in language. . . . Many were less than convinced that all students can learn; they voiced the view that they should be kind and considerate to all, but they accepted as fact the theory that some simply cannot learn" (p. 264).

For Goodlad and many other educators, the belief that the disadvantaged merely have deficient learning skills is a destructive legacy in American schooling. Says Goodlad:

Society's moral shortcomings lie primarily in grossly mis-understanding what our schools are for and underestimating what is required of those who are their daily stewards. The school system's moral delinquency is in structuring the enterprise in ways that deny students access to the knowl-edge they need. All students are disadvantaged, some — largely those who are poor and from minority groups — are disadvantaged more than others. The most compelling moral imperatives for teachers pertain to their necessary vigilance in ensuring that their school fulfills its designated functions well and equitably and to the nature of the unique relation-ship between the teacher and the taught. (pp. 52-53)

In Spring Branch's battle for all children to learn, there is no room for equivocation. The "old ways" are being thrown out. Period. This, according to Stevens, is "absolutely frightening to many."

"Individual efficacious behavior is what we're going for in this district," explains Stevens. "Every worker, regardless of where they are, is required to take ownership. If you slough off, you're not doing your job. We're all interdependently related to the whole mission of teaching all children in this district. You can't isolate yourself in the classroom. Those days are over. And it's frightening people to death."

The Role of Brain-Compatible Learning

Stevens also has brought a new vitality to teaching by intro-ducing what the district leaders believe is a superior teaching tool: brain-compatible learning. At its simplest, brain-compatible learning is what John Dewey talked about a century ago: the process of making connections between teaching and the physi-ology of the human brain.

The studies of brain-compatible learning reveal a matrix that can be placed not just over a classroom, but over an entire school. Although every brain is unique — and the more we learn, the more unique we become — the basic functioning of the brain is the same in all of us. The analogy could be that we know how the muscles and nerves operate to move an eyelid up and down and how the eye transmits signals through the optic nerve to the brain, but how each of us views and interprets what we see is unique. Brain-based learning tosses out much of the traditional lore of teaching. In its purest application, it requires restructuring how classrooms and schools are organized and similarly changing testing and grading policies.

Understanding effective brain functions is a first step. The human brain works best when the individual feels no undue stress from any physical, emotional, or psychological threat and when there are interactions that involve emotions, memory systems, and intrinsic and extrinsic motivation as part of learning. The brain's requirement of three interactive elements — relaxed alertness, immersion, and active processing — is a commonsense cornerstone.

Relaxed alertness is the brain's state when the individual feels most safe. Within this comfort zone, the individual may "safely" be challenged to think, to push thoughts beyond the routine or the expected. *Immersion* calls for the integration of the curriculum and the application of learning to personal knowledge and experience. In short, the thinking must have relevance. *Active processing* takes this relevance a step further, allowing the student to take charge of the meaning and to search for broader implications. The application of brain-compatible learning for educators gives a new meaning to the phrase, "owning the curriculum."

Two leaders in the application of brain functioning to instructional technique are Renate Caine and Geoffrey Caine. In *Making Connections: Teaching and the Human Brain* (1991), they listed 12 "simple and neurologically sound" principles:

1. The brain is a parallel processor, bringing together thoughts, emotions, and behaviors.
2. Learning engages the entire physiology.
3. The search for meaning — making sense of experience — is innate.

4. The search for meaning occurs through patterning, bringing together the scientist and the artist and resisting the meaningless.
5. Emotions are critical to patterning.
6. The two hemispheres — right brain/left brain — are inextricably interactive.
7. Learning involves both focused attention and peripheral perception.
8. Learning involves both conscious and unconscious processes.
9. We have two memory systems, spatial and rote.
10. The brain understands and remembers best when facts and skills are embedded in natural, spatial memory.
11. Learning is enhanced by challenge and inhibited by threat.
12. Each brain is unique. (pp. 80-87)

The implications of these principles applied to the classroom are profound. At the heart of the theory is the principle that the finest learning process is that which involves the child directly, has relevance to his or her life, and inspires more learning. The learning process itself cannot take place unless the child feels safe. The child will not learn — beyond mechanical memorization, and certainly not comprehensively — unless the child sees an application to his or her life. And no child is going to learn unless he or she believes that the learning is valuable.

For some teachers, brain-based learning poses difficulties because it requires direct interaction, often a personal interaction, with the student. To the teacher who prefers to stand in front of the classroom and lecture, this tightening of the teacher-student bond can be a problem. It also is difficult for the teacher who does not believe that all children *can* learn. Brain-based learning not only reinforces teaching so that all children will learn, it also provides the physiological and psychological means to that end. Its central objective is to move from memorization of information to meaningful learning and long-term application. Thus many teachers throughout the country are turning to brain-compatible learning.

Bringing Brain-Compatible Learning to the Spring Branch Effective Schools Process

In Spring Branch, the teachers began their staff development with basic brain physiology and then applied it to their own knowledge. Perhaps the most important element of brain-compatible learning is the affirmation of the child's personal worth. Judy Stevens comments:

> Children come to us like butterflies. When they get here on the first day of school, a four-year-old, five-year-old, they think they can hang the moon. If they stay in our system, not just Spring Branch, any educational system, up through the years, and they get to 12th grade, even our best graduates, they're more like a cocoon than when they came in. We stifle their curiosity. We just about nail them to their chairs; we tell them to be quiet; and we tell them this is what they're going to do and how, and no more and no less. And we don't support them, value them, nurture them. For some, we decide early on that because Mommy's a drug user or Daddy's not around that they're not of value. We don't expect too much. We don't believe. We don't encourage. We don't let them learn with their friends, and we decide what's important, doling out the chosen facts that will cause them to fill out the ditto pages "correctly" so the teacher looks acceptable and collects the check. Not here. Not anymore. Not in Spring Branch. We will not revert our butterflies back into their cocoons. We have the tools to make them stronger, more valuable, more beautiful butterflies.

The change that Spring Branch is seeking goes to the very foundation of public education. Stevens admits that there are people who would like to see her, Effective Schools, and brain-compatible learning go away. What Spring Branch is trying to halt is the abusive or punitive way children are taught. Stevens is not saying that people fell into this abusive mode intentionally. She points out that much of our way of teaching is based on how the monks taught the classics back in the 16th century. Perhaps that worked in the 16th century when we still believed the world had some flat, square edges. But in an era when imaging devices can photograph the brain and show how it responds under stimulation, the old ways of teaching children are no longer valid. In fact, some would argue that, given what we now know about teaching and learning, those old ways are unconscionable, even criminal.

Brain-compatible learning also affects professional development. As Caine and Caine (1991) commented:

> We should remember, incidentally, that adults involved with schools are equally affected. Our territory, behavior, security, groups, and rituals are also being challenged. We could therefore expect adults to downshift and respond to problems in ways that are also deeply ingrained. This is often how adults in schools deal with "maintaining discipline." (p. 68)

Thus maintaining classroom discipline often is reduced to systematic rewards and punishments. Brain research points out that "extrinsic motivation inhibits intrinsic motivation. In other words, a system of rewards and punishment can be selectively demotivating in the long term . . . it reduces the desire as well as the capacity of learners to engage in original thought" (Caine and Caine 1991, pp. 71-72).

Typical systems of rewards and punishments injure the intellectual development of children, because the traditional atmosphere of the classroom is threatening to most children, causing their learning capacity to downshift.

As teachers gain insights into brain-compatible teaching and learning, they can move beyond the limits of the immediate classroom. "Once you understand the theory and look around at your school," insists Stevens, "you know you have to change curriculum, instruction, and assessment. The schools are in trouble. All schools, even those who think they're doing a good job, are in trouble. We're not extending the learning process to millions of kids. If you're not just diabolical, you know you have to change something."

Stevens has solid support for her innovations from Hal Guthrie, superintendent of the Spring Branch Independent School District, who brought in the Effective Schools Process. "Dr. Judy Stevens came to us already as an 'Effective' administrator," explained Guthrie. "Now she has found the research and data to improve student achievement. But instead of us in the central office doing the usual military style, top down, this is what you are going to do, she has brought the teachers and coordinators together and said, 'OK, here's the new literature. I think it can really help us, but I want to know what you think'."

Collaborative leadership is not a new management style in business, but it is new in the hierarchical structure of the public schools. Stevens has used this collaboration to buttress a voluntary approach. In 1992, she realized the potential for brain-based learning, but she also realized that bringing the school system around to it would be a Herculean task. She immediately decided to take a year to study brain compatibility and how it applies to an integrated curriculum.

"We're talking about changing the whole nature of the classroom. No more punitive behavior. No more being abusive to children. This requires teachers to be actively involved in the learning process of children," says Stevens. "And make no mistake about it, it is much, much easier to teach the other way."

Stevens set up study groups across the district. She flooded them with the research, stunned personally by the abundance of it and how it had been ignored by most educators. "Masses of educators just pushed this aside," says Stevens. "And those were the masses who were — and are — training us."

Much of our present understanding of learning comes from the Skinner theory of stimulus and response. The new research shows that this theory is flawed when applied to human learning behavior. Individuals must create their own motivation. Once a child "owns" his or her motivation, then learning becomes continuous and long-term. Goodlad, Glasser, Sizer, Comer, and others agree that the need for a new pedagogy involving brain research is not being addressed because it would radically change what is currently being done in most classrooms.

As Stevens continues to expand the knowledge base throughout Spring Branch, she is finding increased numbers of teachers desiring information and instruction on creating brain-compatible classrooms. Study groups flourish; and though participation is voluntary, principals are encouraging their teachers to take advantage of the workshops.

Empowerment and Learning

"Our principal [Linda Reed] gives us the power to really use our site-based management. It's not just a slogan here as it is in other schools, other districts," says Lynda Sullivan, a teacher at Spring Shadows Elementary School in the Spring Branch district. "We don't all come from the same thought processes or the same background. Just like our kids, we sit here as teachers and work it out. Together. We talk, we compromise. How do we put it together so it is the best for the children? We were not given that power in the past. We were told by the district what worked, what to do. Now they turn to us and say, 'What's working? What are you learning?' And they support us. Unbelievable, but true."

Sullivan, whose classroom has become a realistic rain forest created by her students, believes strongly that she has become more effective as a teacher because of brain-compatible learning. She knows — intuitively, as well as from research — that creating a safe environment for her students is the vital first step.

"At the beginning of the year, I tell them, 'This is your home away from home. We are family. And we will treat each other with love and with respect and with kindness. You may expect that from me just as I expect you to show it to each other.' And that's the way it is all year round." Sullivan adds that the same idea of respect guides the faculty and administration in their dealings.

"The other key is that when you can teach this way, they stay so busy, and they stay so involved and so interested, that they don't have time to think about misbehaving," notes Sullivan. "I think a lot of times — and this has been proven now — that when we have behavior problems it is because children are bored. Kids are bright. All kids. They're going to use their intelligence one way or another. It's okay if they're not perfect on everything. And that's what I say to them."

The change brought by the Effective Schools Process and the new instructional techniques has benefited not only the teachers and students in Spring Branch, but also the parents.

"I have parents in my room a lot. I love parents," says Sullivan. "Parents are a wonderful resource; and I think the fact that they feel welcome in the school goes back to the Effective Schools, the knowledge that they know that we believe in their children and in them. Just come on in. And they know that they can come into my room and say, 'But I don't know a lot about photosynthesis.' And I say, 'You don't need to. Come on in. The kids will show you what it's all about, and I would love to have you helping us do this or do that.' So they're welcome here and they're excited. And it makes the kids feel better. School's a fun place to be, and we all care about each other."

Since Spring Branch began the Effective Schools Process, there has been no shortage of workshops, seminars, and lectures on subjects ranging from ability tracking to math for kindergartners. They are open to all — teacher, principal, staff. Veteran teacher Margaret Rife combines the research on Effective Schools directly with the new teaching options.

"The correlates are the key. Every school system should do these. The basic tenet, all children can learn, must be at your core," Rife insists. "When you look at that child whom you're having trouble with, you think, 'Okay, this is going to be the one who can't.' But you remember, all children can learn. I have it posted in my room. I believe in it so thoroughly and the children always, always prove it."

Rife explains how she attended one of the classes on how the different parts of the brain become involved in the learning process. For the first time she saw proof that if she involved the child's various senses, the child's emotions, and the child's prior experiences, she could greatly enhance that child's learning. She remembers how she used to have the children just memorize the original American Colonies. She shakes her head in disapproval at how she could expect them to find value in that disjointed learning process.

"Now I explain not only how those Colonies differ from what they know today, but how some of the same things that were important in New England are important today in Texas." When learning the names of the Colonies, the students also clap and recite. Says Rife: "It sounds Mickey Mouse, but it does actually help. You're saying it, you're physically adding to it, and you're looking at the teacher, so you're using your visual senses."

Effective Schools encourages teachers to explore new learning strategies. But teachers, especially more experienced teachers, are not always comfortable making those decisions.

"There's no doubt some teachers are very reluctant to take more responsibility, to be empowered," says Susan Saied, a math specialist at Nottingham Elementary in Spring Branch. "They want to be told what to do, because that's comfortable and safe. But once you realize that power gives you more control, your own destiny, you can take your children further. There's no stopping any teacher then."

"When teachers are empowered, I don't have to be the one that makes sure everybody teaches for the sake of the children. The people around them will do that," explains Linda Reed, principal of Spring Shadows. "A team will make the other people on that team be strong or make them make the choice to not be a teacher on this campus. In a truly Effective School, teachers see exactly what the instructional focus is all about. They see the different kinds of research, the database behind programs that work. And you let teachers play that out. And the teacher next door sees, 'Hey, this is working, these children are learning to read.' So that teacher goes for the training, and soon she has it in her classroom. It's infectious. Soon you have the whole school moving in the same direction, doing what needs to be done."

Judy Stevens and her colleagues admit that change often is still a battle. But, Stevens says, the only way the children will grow is if the teachers and administrators grow.

"I believe that with Effective Schools and its continuing growth, with all the research and training we are doing, that we have the opportunity here to create something that could have an over-whelming impact on our state, on our nation, if not our world. We are a microcosm of America, and we have the will to see that all children can learn. And in order for people to support public schools in the way we have to support them to maintain our democracy, they've got to see it can work. It's the vision idea. Everywhere else they see the status quo. Here they see the future, because these committed people believe that all children are worth saving and we are giving them the skills to accomplish that."

Chapter 4

Changing the Culture
of Schools

In order for the Effective Schools Process to permeate a school system, it must change the basic culture of the schools. Without such broad change, the classroom changes described in the previous chapter will become isolated and eventually the benefits obtained will wither away.

In the late 1970s and early 1980s a knowledge explosion occurred around the concept of organizational learning, which was defined as a group process within the organization by which the organization's members come to understand the relationship between their actions and corporate outcomes (Duncan and Weiss 1979). Researchers began to realize that new organizational structures are not likely to be reliable until an organization's culture is changed to support the new framework of ideas. Certainly institutionalization of these changes would not occur. In schools, once the innovative instructional leader left, the school usually would fall back into old ways of operating and teachers would revert to the status quo.

The concept of culture is "rooted more in theories of group dynamics and group growth than in anthropological theories of how large cultures evolve," says Edgar Schein (1985). He continues:

> When we study organizations, we do not have to decipher a completely strange language or set of customs and mores. Rather, our problem is to distinguish — within a broader host culture — the unique features of a particular social unit

in which we are interested. This social unit often will have a history that can be deciphered, and the key actors in the formation of that culture can often be studied, so that we are not limited, as the anthropologist is often limited, by the lack of historical data.

Because we are looking at evolving social units within a larger host culture, we also can take advantage of learning theories and develop a dynamic concept of organizational culture. Culture is learned, evolves with new experiences, and can be changed if one understands the dynamics of the learning process. If one is concerned about managing or changing culture, one must look to what we know about the learning and unlearning of complex beliefs and assumptions that underlie social behavior. (p. 8)

Thus school culture is defined in three sectors: the classroom, the school, and the district. However, these three distinct cultures must be very similar to each other, without much deviation in values between classrooms or schools, in order to have the district as a whole participate fully in the Effective Schools Process.

Shared Values, Shared Vision

Shared values are at the heart of the Effective Schools philosophy. At the individual school level, we ask these questions:

1. Is the Effective Schools philosophy permeating the school?
2. Are the systems within the school effectively responding to external and internal events in accordance with that philosophy?
3. Are the systems stable? Are the school's organizational functions and feedback mechanisms balanced? Is the school responding to classroom data?
4. When problems arise, are teachers, parents, principal, students, and support staff ready and able to solve them?

The most important criterion is effectiveness. In the Effective Schools philosophy, usually articulated in a school's mission statement, that criterion is: "All children *can* learn, and so all children *will* learn." That criterion determines how frameworks will be drawn so that teachers and administrators make the best decisions, and thus change gains momentum. Without the criterion of effectiveness — by which all decisions are made, all actions are carried out, all programs are evaluated — there is no adequate basis for shared values.

Some of the shared values that flow from this criterion are:

- Celebrating growth and change.
- Respecting individuals.
- Holding high expectations for students and educators.
- Encouraging risk taking.
- Recognizing educators as professionals.
- Holding everyone accountable for success.
- Using opportunity-to-learn pedagogy.
- Analyzing and refining curricula continuously.
- Encouraging collaboration and collegiality.

In many Effective Schools the school culture changes first at the margins, until one day there is a critical mass of teachers and students who seem to "take hold" of the philosophy. Then the old school culture decomposes, and the new school culture blossoms. In Effective Schools, we see new actions taking place and new beliefs entering the school culture, unfreezing the culture for change. Then, building block by building block, the culture is reconstructed but in a new configuration. The "refreezing" — in the Effective Schools context — never totally takes place, because the school now believes in continual renewal and improvement and has institutionalized the process of change.

Cultural change does not take place quickly or without many hours spent in professional development by all persons involved in school reform. One of the big mistakes often made by school policy makers and university gurus is to underestimate the needed amount of staff development. A culture changes slowly and by stages. First, patterns of communications within the school and district must change. Then coordination needs to become smoother and more complete. Finally, a monitoring system, developed over the entire organizational change process, must be refined and routinely used. Feedback from such monitoring becomes the basis of new plans and ongoing change in the learning community.

If this sequence is not followed and educators are not aware of the need for attention to the tenets of successful change, schools very often will have to backtrack and deal with cultural change in the developmental sequence specified here and described by several researchers (Huberman and Miles 1984; Taylor 1984; Fullan 1993).

Effective Schools and Other Reforms

The Effective Schools philosophy is distinctive because it is comprehensive. Other reform processes tend to be too limited to effectively change school culture. A summary may be helpful in understanding this feature. Following are a few examples of other reform processes and the difficulties they encounter.

Sizer's Coalition of Essential Schools (CES), after seven years of attempting to implement their Nine Principles in high schools across the United States, has had limited success in changing the classroom behaviors of teachers and students or in curriculum development (Muncey and McQuillan 1993). No student achievement gains have been documented, and yet an impressive national organization exists, ready to "scale up."

CES is aware of teachers' need for cultural change in the workplace. In fact, the Nine Principles contain many cultural as well as pedagogical components. But CES did not train for cultural change or even promote such change. Therefore, the teachers in the CES schools were left to attempt to redesign their curricula by following a content-full but process-deficient program. The Coalition of Essential Schools spent more than $100 million in 10 years (1985-1995) on slightly more than 300 schools nationwide and had no school effects and few program effects to show for it. The success of CES has much to do with the charismatic leadership of Sizer and his strong fundraising and organizational abilities.

In spite of this, membership in the Coalition is increasing every year. (The average grant to schools to adopt the Coalition's program is $250,000 a year.) Five hundred new schools joined CES in the past two years (1993-95). Sizer, who commissioned a rigorous evaluation of CES in 1990 (Muncey and McQuillan 1993), is now developing a change process as a result of that evaluation. Most of Muncey and McQuillan's findings agree with those of the school effectiveness literature; therefore, the new CES process probably will turn out to look very much like the one designed by Effective Schools.

The School Development Program of James Comer paid attention to cultural change in schools. Although the Comer Process — called the School Development Program — is more an excellent research project than a school reform process, educators are learning a great deal about positive and negative school and teacher effects on certain inner-city students through Comer's work. The Comer Process "grew up" about the time Effective Schools Research was discovering the correlates (1970-1978). Although there are many similarities in the work of James Comer and that of Ronald Edmonds, their emphases, development, and mode of demonstration were slightly different (NCESRD 1989). Comer originally emphasized principles of child development in the training of administrators, parents, and teachers in changing the school climate: process over substance. Edmonds emphasized skills of restructuring and a new belief system about the educability of all children: substance over process. Now both the Comer model and the Effective Schools Process have important process components as well as substance (restructuring) components.

Slavin's "Success for All" uses some of the cultural tenets of the Effective Schools Research. (Slavin was director of the National Center for Effective Elementary Schools at Johns Hopkins University from 1985 until 1990.) Although Slavin's program is only four years old, already he has carefully documented successes in most of the schools with which he is working. Success for All is prescriptive and top-down and considers only curricula, instructional methods, and "other pragmatic components that could be easily reproduced in various settings." The program emphasizes a pre-reading curriculum (preschool and kindergarten) and a new reading curriculum for Grades 1 and 2. Slavin hopes to demonstrate that by front loading resources in intensive and preventative instruction, students will not develop the deficiencies and learning gaps that are characteristic of at-risk students.

Henry Levin's "Accelerated Schools," which now reaches approximately 700 school communities in 34 states, shares much in common with Effective Schools. Primary is the belief that children, regardless of race and socioeconomic background, can learn and succeed in school. Accelerated Schools emphasizes student achievement and learning, enriched curriculum and instruction, family and community involvement, and improvements in school climate.

However, the philosophies of Effective Schools and Accelerated Schools differ in their approach to the change process. Where the Effective Schools Process is guided by a powerful and growing research base on school effectiveness, the Accelerated Schools process is guided by an equally powerful constructivist approach that focuses on helping each school community to develop policies and programs that are consistent with that community's unique needs and cultures. An Accelerated Schools coach is needed to implement the first year of the change program, and decisions about change involve the entire school community.

The National Center for the Accelerated Schools Project is located at Stanford University. There are 10 regional centers and more than 200 trainers.

National Center for Restructuring Education, Schools, and Teaching (NCREST) and the Center for School Reform, Teacher's College, New York City. In an attempt to bring together all people involved in the various facets of school reform — teachers, administrators, policy makers, parents, and community organizers — NCREST was formed in 1990. NCREST documents learner-centered schools and change processes; develops and disseminates information about promising practices; translates research into policy and professional development initiatives; organizes conferences, meetings, and networks that connect school reformers in many roles; and manages an electronic network that links practitioners and researchers. NCREST is organized around their own specific initiatives and works collaboratively with other organizations, such as the United Federation of Teachers (UFT), the Center for Collaborative Education, and the New York City Board of Education. Their documentation shows a number of beneficial outcomes in terms of changed school structures and improved student performance. NCREST also is interested in engaging in policy development and professional development congruent with their findings.

Most of NCREST's work builds on early school effectiveness research, and their expertise will be helpful in documenting successful change strategies. They also hope to create new curricula for undergraduate and graduate teacher education.

Spady's Outcome-Based Education is a "spinoff" of the Effective Schools Process "frequent monitoring" correlate. Most Effective Schools educators view OBE as too top-down; however, OBE often is used in concert with the Effective Schools Process for more beneficial results.

The reason for going into this elaboration of the results of several reform programs now being implemented is to draw to the reader's attention the importance of cultural change in organizations when attempting to redesign and reform them. As Schein (1985) suggests:

> Many organization change programs that are labeled as involving "culture change" actually deal only with this one element of the culture — the measurements to be applied in

the future. Thus, new chief executives come in and announce that they will emphasize product quality, or bring costs under control, or get the organization to be more customer oriented.

This sometimes sounds like a real change in mission but, on closer examination, turns out merely to be a new focus on how to measure success. From this perspective it is clear that such new signals are only one element of culture change. If only the results signals are changed, without concern for mission, goals, and means, very little actual change may come about. Consensus must be achieved both on the criteria and on the means by which information is to be gathered. (p. 62)

From these brief descriptions alone, it is relatively easy to see that some programs place more emphasis than others on processes that change school cultures. Often, the missing element, Schein suggests, is "consensus on the criteria and other means by which information [for making decisions] is gathered."

Ted Sizer recently announced that schools must be changed "one school at a time." He is right. Edmonds knew this in 1976 when he began planning and implementing a school improvement project in schools in New York City. Carl Marburger knew that educators had to change one school at a time in 1980 and wrote a book on school-based management in 1985 outlining the process and training necessary to bring about shared decision-making at the school site. Even Herbert J. Klausmeier and colleagues, authors of Individually Guided Education (IGE), were convinced that schools had to have instruction and research (I&R) units and instructional improvement committees (IIC) in order to change successfully (Taylor and Levine 1991). Unfortunately, in the mid-1960s, when Klausmeier was developing IGE, there was no research on site-based management to which to refer. In his work, Klausmeier anticipated all of the components of the Effective Schools Process except the setting of missions, goals, and restructuring strategies at the school level. (These are "school effects"; IGE primarily emphasized "teacher effects.") No emphasis was given to culture change.

Stages of Culture Change

The first stage, when change is introduced, is one of anxiety. Common language, shared values, and consensus are most important during the first days and months of culture change. In this first stage, the most important factor for success is encouragement, along with solid help from school administrators and central office personnel. The working relationship between the central office and the schools, still evolving at this stage, is critical.

The new culture "takes over" during the second stage. Concerns about the new organizational arrangements begin to diminish. School board members, the superintendent, principals, and teachers learn together and grow together in the new culture. It is during this second stage that most of the restructuring takes place. Those promoting school reform catch the vision, remove the most severe obstacles to reform, and design the new school and its operations. The working relationship between the principal and the teachers is transformed during this stage, and school leadership becomes pervasive (Taylor 1984).

The third stage is actualization, when the culture has been significantly transformed and is open to further change as a process of discovery and revision becomes the cultural norm. Indicators of teacher-student interaction in the classroom evidence cultural and pedagogical change.

In stages two and three of the Effective Schools Process, emphasis is on monitoring and feedback, continuously gathering data for making decisions in the classroom, the grade level, the school, and the district. Teachers and principals learn how to gather good data and how to interpret and use the data in their daily routines.

In 1987, Jacob Stampen wrote an article comparing Total Quality Management and Effective Schools Research in which he said:

> Purkey and Smith's (1983) list of research needs in the school effectiveness area provides a good indication of what is not being done. They list the following as priority needs: (a) longitudinal studies tracking school and student perfor-

mance over time, (b) studies investigating processes associated with effectiveness, and (c) studies of successful goal definition and implementation.

The question remains about where and how to begin the task of associating statistical control with educational administration at the institutional level. A logical place to be begin would be within schools. (1987, p. 430)

Stampen felt that software that helped educators at the school site to analyze data using statistical methods would help a great deal 1) to make decisions regarding curriculum and student performance, and 2) to understand the organizational and pedagogical processes that produced those data. Stampen continued:

The role of the master teacher in Deming's system now becomes clear. The master teacher really is a personification of the function of designing a data base and ensuring that all contributors to the production process have appropriate statistical tools. Another function is to determine whether organizational actions influence quality in a systematic way. If quality is not improving, they can re-examine the factors affecting success and renew their efforts to influence those factors in the desired direction. The essential point here, however, is that statistical techniques are not enough. The data and analysis have to be anchored within a particular environment so that (holding environmental factors constant) systematic relationships can be identified and monitored over time. (p. 430)

Today, nearly a decade after the publication of Stampen's article, software programs are available for gathering, interpreting, and applying sampling and other statistical procedures to data in individual schools. One such software program is the Management Information System for Effective Schools (MISES) created by Don McIsaac at the National Center for Effective Schools Research and Development. The Effective Schools Process creates the particular environment that the data and analysis must be anchored in, so that systemic relationships can be identified and monitored over time.

Schein (1985), in his analysis of organizational culture, explained:

> What we need to understand, then, is how the *individual* intentions of the founders, leaders, or conveners of a new group or organization, their own definitions of the situation, their assumptions and values, come to be a *shared, consensually validated* set of definitions that are passed on to new members as the correct way to define the situation. These intentions and definitions, as they exist consciously or not in the leader's mind, can always be analyzed into an external and an internal set of issues. The external issues have to do with the leader's and the group's definition of the environment and how to survive in it; the internal issues have to do with the leader's and the group's definition of how to organize relationships among the members of the group to permit survival in the defined environment through effective performance and the creation of internal comfort.
>
> Although these issues are highly interdependent in practice, for purposes of analysis, it is important to note that they reflect very different sets of functional imperatives. The external issues are concerned with survival in what must be assumed to be a real environment that is, in part, beyond the control of group members. These external realities define the basic mission, primary task, or core functions of the group. The group must then figure out how to accomplish the core mission, how to measure its accomplishment, and how to maintain its success in the face of a changing environment. But survival over any length of time requires internal integration, and such integration is, of course, aided by external success. (pp. 50-51)

Making Change Stick

Educators cannot bring about lasting change in school culture unless they also change district and state policies to bring them into alignment with the new school culture and the new school policies that support that culture. If a district or state wishes to sabotage school reform efforts, it easily can do so. Risks are high in any culture change process. Many schools and districts, when they are on the verge of adopting the Effective Schools Process, lose a superintendent or some effective principals or two or three "reform-minded" members of the school board, and practices and procedures fall back on business as usual.

Without real culture change at the policy and procedure levels — usually outside the individual school — new practices may be lost because they may be "too risky" for teachers and building-level administrators. For real change to stick, principals and teachers must be supported in their quest for new ways to reach and teach all children no matter who is in charge. The commitment to Effective Schools must be pervasive at all levels, which means that the commitment to deep culture change must be translated into practical policies and procedures.

Again, Schein (1985) leads us to recognize the necessity of shared understandings:

> The shared values of the new learning community must be explicit. Unless the assumptions, language, and criteria of effectiveness are made abundantly clear at all levels, leaders who attempt to change the school culture will see their efforts stagnate or, worse, will watch those efforts result in chaos.
>
> Because culture is a dynamic process, the best way to understand it is to draw on group and leadership theory where such theory has dealt specifically with how new organizations form. We must pay special attention to the role of entrepreneurs, founders, and leaders who manage key organizational transitions. And we must draw on dynamic theories of group development. . . .
>
> The process of culture formation is, in a sense, identical with the process of group formation in that the very essence of "groupness" or group identity — the shared patterns of thought, belief, feelings, and values that result from shared experience and common learning — is what we ultimately end up calling the "culture" of that group. Without a group,

there can be no culture; and without some degree of culture, we really are talking about only an aggregate of individuals, not a group. So group growth and culture formation can be seen as two sides of the same coin, and both are the result of leadership activities. Both are also essential to making change stick in Effective Schools. (p. 50)

Chapter 5

Curriculum Development, Student Assessment, Staff Development, and Accountability

Chapters 3 and 4 examined the philosophical and practical under-pinnings of Effective Schools. If classrooms and schools change fundamentally, as we illustrated in Chapter 3, then the Effective Schools Process can produce a wave of change that will ripple through the district. Changing the classroom ultimately can presage changing how superintendents and central office administrators operate, how principals exercise leadership, how school boards function, and how parents and other community members invest themselves and their resources in education.

In Chapter 4, we broadened our focus to examine why the basic culture of a school — and, in turn, a district — must be transformed. We said that the Effective Schools Process must permeate a school system, or else the changes in classrooms will become isolated and eventually will simply wither away.

In this chapter, we examine some of the specific emphases of the Effective Schools Process, namely, curriculum development, student assessment, staff development, and accountability. By attending to these specific areas, educators increase the likelihood that basic change at the classroom level and more pervasive cultural change throughout a school and district will root, grow, and ultimately flourish.

For the last several years many states have been attempting to align state school codes, education policy, and assessment or oversight procedures with Effective Schools and school effectiveness research.* Among the most active of these states are Ohio, Nebraska, Kansas, Florida, Michigan, Maryland, Arkansas, Kentucky, Washington, Oregon, Connecticut, New Hampshire, Vermont, Virginia, North Carolina, South Carolina, Mississippi, and Louisiana.

Specific training in the Effective Schools Process and complementary change processes is under way in New Hampshire, New York, Vermont, Connecticut, Virginia, Louisiana, Washington, Oregon, Colorado, California, Texas, New Jersey, South Carolina, North Carolina, and Hawaii. Various schools and districts — in some cases, the entire state system — have developed as models of the Effective Schools Process and the comprehensive application of school effectiveness research findings for some years. A few have done so for more than a decade.

However, most states, including those listed in the previous paragraphs, are struggling to match policies that govern their supervision of schools — including state-level work in curriculum policy, student assessment, staff development, and accountability — with the most recent indicators of school effectiveness. Without such congruence, the Effective Schools picture is incomplete.

"What gets measured gets done" is a simple maxim in school life. And what gets done fills the school day. Therefore, what states set as curricular criteria and standards for assessment, in large measure, determines what and how teachers teach.

Unfortunately, in most public school districts today, there is little or no congruence between state policies and what Effective Schools Research — and the practical experience of many Effective Schools models — shows ought to be done in order to create the greatest measure of success for all students. Indeed,

---

*"School effectivenss research" refers to early effective schools research and subsequent studies done predominately by university researchers. Effective Schools Research (capitalized) subsumes this body of research and adds studies done by applied researchers. The term is capitalized to indicate the body of research espoused by the National Center for Effective Schools. The Effective Schools Process was developed from this research base.

state policies and regulations — and working conditions as specified in teachers' contracts — often are anachronistic, out of touch with recent research on school effectiveness, and therefore counterproductive to school reform.

As much for this reason as for any other, many of today's teachers continue to teach in ways that are outmoded and have been shown to be ineffective. They too often teach a curriculum that is outdated and out of touch with the need's of today's young learners — and the needs of future workers. Student achievement continues to be "measured" in ways that are disconnected from the curriculum that the students experience and says little about whether students can use their knowledge and skills in real-world contexts. Teachers' knowledge and instruction techniques fall short of current needs because school, district, and state education leaders spend too little time and effort on staff development and retraining. And, finally, few adequate measures of accountability are available to link teacher and administrator performance to either further professional development or rewards for a job well done.

Educators in Effective Schools know that an essential feature for success is the linkage of curriculum development, student assessment, staff development, and accountability. This linkage is absolutely necessary so that teachers and administrators have the support necessary for them to work effectively. The shared vision and shared values of Effective Schools cannot be sustained without the strong chain of these elements girding up the day-to-day work in schools, classrooms, and board rooms.

The Fallacy of "Loose Coupling"

Karl Weick (1979) set off an avalanche when he described school organizations as "loosely coupled." By "loosely coupled," he meant that because of present organizational arrangements and cultural beliefs, change will require "time to ramify and ramifications will be weak." In other words, the first stages of change may contain actions (such as reorientation of school governance to school-based management) whose consequences are not fully realized until much later (pp. 110-12).

Many researchers grabbed the term "loosely coupled" and, just as they later would swarm around the concept of organizational culture, swept logic aside to interpret loose coupling as an expression of the relationship between curriculum, assessment, staff development, and accountability. In fact, by wholly misinterpreting Weick, they justified incongruence. This justification let them off the hook. It justified incongruence as acceptable, as a "normal" state of affairs during the process of change.

In fact, Weick believed that some form of loose coupling was advantageous to the creative and autonomous decision making demanded by teachers in the delivery of instruction. He felt that loose coupling allowed "rapid adaptation to shifting conditions." However, he did not say that it was a goal or a static condition. Indeed, Weick criticized schools for being loosely coupled and blamed a "status quo mentality" in schools on the fact that results of teaching and learning were seldom assessed. When they were assessed — for instance, by using standardized, norm-referenced tests twice a year — the test results were given to the principal and teachers six weeks later with no direction about how to respond. This delay in feedback is strong evidence of a very loosely coupled organization. It also is evidence of a weak connection between assessment and a commitment to high academic achievement for all students.

If what gets measured gets done, then it makes sense that what gets measured should be an important focus during any change process. What gets measured establishes the criteria and standards for what really counts. What really counts in changing a school organization are the shared values, the vision, and the mission of the stakeholders in the school. Loose coupling may allow for creativity and growth, but it is not a "normal" or constant state, as some have interpreted the term. In fact, when loose coupling becomes the norm, then the system — and the change process — is likely to be dysfunctional.

Collaboration, Consensus, and Group Learning

What gets measured must come from the consensus on shared values and how those values are to be translated into a vision and a mission. State school codes, district policies, and school policies need to be carefully aligned. For that to happen, curriculum development, student and program assessment, staff development, and accountability must be linked together at the school site and at the district level. And the process should occur in a bottom-up fashion, where consensus emerges at the grassroots and enlarges "upward" to draw in the wider circle of stakeholders.

At the same time, we realize that the social, economic, and political environment outside the school will determine possibilities, options, and constraints and thus shape the school's tasks for bringing about real change. This means that every school and district must develop a vision of what it wants to be in the face of external conditions or problems that, in the end, may temper its ambitions. Schein (1985) describes five problems inherent in adapting to external conditions in order for the school's focus, or shared values, to survive and become operational:

> 1. *Mission and Strategy.* Obtaining a shared understanding of core mission, primary task, manifest and latent functions.
> 2. *Goals.* Developing consensus on goals, as derived from the core mission.
> 3. *Means.* Developing consensus on the means to be used to attain the goals, such as the organization structure, division of labor, reward system, and authority system.
> 4. *Measurement.* Developing consensus on the criteria to be used in measuring how well the group is doing in fulfilling its goals, such as the information and control system.
> 5. *Correction.* Developing consensus on the appropriate remedial or repair strategies to be used if goals are not being met. (p. 52)

From this perspective, organizational learning (or group learning) for the members of the group — initially, at least teachers, administrators, parents, and students — is a key to forming a common base of information on which to build consensus, first of all, and subsequently to enlarge that consensus among the broader constituency, including policy makers at increasingly distant (or "higher") levels.

Collaboration in Action in Spring Branch

We turn again, as we did in Chapter 3, to Spring Branch, Texas, as an illustration of such collaboration in action. Four categories of organizational actions make up the Collaborative Curriculum Development (CCD) process in the Spring Branch elementary schools, according to Judy Stevens, who directs elementary instruction. These categories parallel the four emphases stated in the title of this chapter:

1. *Curriculum Development.* This is an interactive, ongoing process that focuses on the importance of developing the philosophy and beliefs of Effective Schools Research as a prerequisite and foundation for the entire curriculum framework. Spring Branch emphasizes that teachers are decision makers whose primary task is to facilitate the development of lifelong learners who are capable of success in the 21st century.
2. *Implementation and Staff Development.* Procedures for implementing CCD are described for teachers, along with the staff development decision-making model created to infuse CCD into the culture of the school and district in order to create change.
3. *Assessment.* The student assessment process for each curriculum framework is described. This assessment process was designed by the teachers and Stevens. Complementing the student assessment process is program evaluation that employs a longitudinal model.
4. *Maintenance, Renewal, and Accountability.* A definition and rationale of continuous renewal is presented. Specific strategies for maintenance and continuous improvement are delineated. Indicators of Effective Schools are enumerated.

Procedures for criteria and standard-setting at individual schools are suggested.

Stevens has formed this integrated system only recently. In designing new organizational arrangements, she and her colleagues (mostly teachers from elementary schools) have put together a concerted chain of functions for carrying out school reform. Stevens feels that these functions must be linked together, or else school reform will bog down every year because one of the "functions" was either counter-productive or simply did not carry out its work, which is to inform teachers and administrators in a timely way of their performance and progress toward school improvement objectives and goals.

Measuring Results

Of all the functions, perhaps the most problematic is assessment, both student assessment and program evaluation. And this function is problematic at all levels, from the classroom to the state.

Schein (1985) points out that once a group (a class of students, for example, or a school's faculty and administration) is performing, it must have consensus on how to judge its own performance in order to know what kind of remedial action to take when things do not go as expected. If members hold widely divergent views of what to look for and how to evaluate the results, they can not develop coordinated remedial action. Thus lack of agreement is often the major source of difficulty in improving performance.

Achieving consensus on evaluation criteria is a complex and often frustrating task. However, by tying together the four functions listed previously, many disagreements can be avoided. Coordinating these functions serves to "synchronize" the individuals' efforts and engender a systemic response, as opposed to potentially disparate individual responses. In this way, problems that are encountered become group problems, rather than individual problems, and can be solved through collaboration and consensus.

Evaluation in applied fields — whether heavy industry, agriculture, health services, or education — must rely on refining and adjusting procedures or processes, not simply assessing products. Schon (1983) calls this reflection-in-action. Implementing the Effective Schools Process involves ongoing process assessment. When a problem occurs during the implementation of a curriculum, for example, teachers must reflect on the problem, diagnose its cause and remedy, and then apply the remedy so that the problem can be solved "on the run."

Practitioners across the country now are designing ongoing, formative evaluation and assessment systems to match the culture and organizational demands of their schools and districts. It is unfortunate that process assessment and evaluation skills are not yet taught in most graduate departments of education administration, curriculum and instruction, or teacher education. These skills are taught in most undergraduate and graduate business and management courses today. Now educators must step forward and claim these tools and better develop them for use in schools and districts. Only by using ongoing assessment tools can teachers be supported in the goal of teaching all children. And only by using the communication channels afforded in curriculum development and staff development will teachers be able to supplement their pedagogical repertoires in a timely way.

Finally, we come to accountability. Stampen (1987) says:

> The role of the master teacher . . . now becomes clear. The master teacher really is a personification of the function of designing a data base and of ensuring that all contributors to the production process have appropriate statistical tools. Another function is to determine whether organizational actions influence quality in a systematic way. If quality is not improving, they can re-examine the factors affecting success and renew their efforts to influence those factors in the desired direction. The essential point here, however, is that statistical techniques are not enough. The data and analysis have to be anchored within a particular environment so that (holding environmental factors constant) sys-

tematic relationships can be identified and monitored over time. (p. 430)

Early on, Edmonds (1979) anticipated the need for an accountability system that included assessment, staff development, and curriculum development components:

> Effective schools get that way partly by making it clear that pupil acquisition of basic school skills takes precedence over all other school activities. When necessary, school energy and resources can be diverted from other business in furtherance of the fundamental objectives. The final effective school characteristic to be set down is that there must be some means by which pupil progress can be frequently monitored. These means may be as traditional as classroom testing on the day's lesson or as advanced as criterion referenced systemwide standardized measures. The point is that some means must exist in the school by which the principal and the teachers remain constantly aware of pupil progress in relationship to instructional objectives. (p. 23)

Professionals are able to hold themselves accountable — and respond to the accountability expectations of their patrons, clients, or constituents — only when the "system" is cohesive. For example, when the shared vision is stated in a mission statement and concrete goals, and assessment is directly linked to the curriculum through which those goals are delivered, then success can be measured. This makes for true and sensible accountability. In many schools and districts such collaboration and consensus still are rare. However, the Effective Schools Process can help educators and others concerned about education to move systematically toward this end. Results from districts such as Spring Branch provide convincing evidence.

Chapter 6

Effective Leaders and What They Do: Four Cases

The backbone of Effective Schools is the moral imperative of teaching so that all children learn. Superintendents recognize that a belief in this imperative is essential to the success of reform. To infuse a school district with this belief and build on it is the on-going task of Effective Schools superintendents and other leaders.

Research and operational data now available demonstrate that the political will and leadership skills exist to create and sustain Effective Schools. School leaders must build on this track record. Many are doing so, because the Effective Schools Process is not just the foundation for change, but a powerful projection into the future of public education.

In our books, *Making School Reform Happen* (Allyn and Bacon 1993) and *Keepers of the Dream* (Excelsior 1994), Effective Schools districts and their leaders were profiled. In this chapter, we present four similar profiles to illustrate what effective leaders do to initiate, sustain, and nurture positive change. Appropriately we begin with Spring Branch, which we have already featured as an example in the preceding chapters.

The Spring Branch, Texas, Experience

Effective Schools leaders have learned the all-important lesson that, in order to propel the improvement process, they must keep their eyes always on the shared vision and keep school employees committed and growing.

Growing is a key word. In order for public education to succeed in the 21st century, it must change how it regards and teaches students. Therein lie both the problem and the solution. Administrators and teachers must be retrained.

Schools are a battlefield for the struggle between old and new ideas and strategies. The field is littered with education and business consultants, gurus, and trainers — all with "the" answer and the requisite publicity and bank balance to prove it. And they are being pushed on districts by city and county leaders, thereby draining scarce funds and demoralizing staffs. They often offer entertainment, not education. Many do more harm than good.

"It's a waste of time that is costing us thousands of children every year and the spirit and talents of hundreds of people who want to see that all children learn, but are stuck working in districts devoid of any sound leadership, that just pander to this hype," says Hal Guthrie, superintendent of the Spring Branch Independent School District in Texas. Guthrie is not one to mince words. But those who have studied the changes he has brought to his 28,000-pupil district near Houston say that he has earned that right.

Spring Branch is a microcosm of America. It had changed from a predominantly white, middle- and upper-class district to one with a fleeing upper class, a shrinking middle class, and an expanding minority and disadvantaged population. Once rated as among the finest districts in the nation, Spring Branch slipped during the 1980s into disrepair, violence, and ineffective, inequitable day-to-day education.

Enter Hal Guthrie. "You have to keep that one value — teaching for learning for all," says Guthrie. "No school system is lost if there is that understanding of true school effectiveness. If there is a genuine, ongoing commitment to the children who go to school, if every superintendent said that our system is going to be one of inclusion rather than exclusion, one where every child learns, where we cut through the excuses, cut through the folklore . . . if every superintendent instilled that one belief system and created an organizational mechanism that allows that belief system to flourish, then those school systems, those children, would not be lost."

Today, the district's test scores and reputation have been revived, and Spring Branch now is regarded as one of the most innovative and productive school districts — for students, faculty, and staff — in the United States. The district management matrix has been completely restructured. Guthrie and his top-notch staff maintain that the success and vitality of the district is because they have kept their eye on the classroom. Their focus is always, unwaveringly, on students.

In establishing one of the most progressive teaching and learning programs in the country — Spring Branch is a leader in brain-compatible teaching strategies — Guthrie has found that the Effective Schools Process he introduced to the district has provided the blueprint for his system's substantive growth.

Hal Guthrie knew when he came into Spring Branch in 1986 from Cedar Rapids, Iowa, that he had to ensure the moral imperative of teaching for learning for all by 1) restructuring the district's organization and management and 2) helping the teachers to become better teachers. He discovered that both tasks involved a learning process that was not only needed but desired. "When I came to the district, teachers and principals were saying, help us, we need knowledge, we need staff development, we need training to deal with a population that we have never seen before," explains Guthrie. "That's where the key was because it was my opportunity then to bring in the school effectiveness concepts — the leadership styles and the expectations primarily. Then we took off."

"Once you have the belief system and you're changing the culture of the organization — that the employees believe and value expectations and student success for all — then you have to develop specific activities around leadership training, around curriculum writing, around focus, climate studies, bring the research to teachers and create a new, solid culture," explains Guthrie. "Now once you have that, you can shift the decision making about what happens on the campus in the areas of curriculum and personnel and organization of the school day to those whom it directly involves and impacts. We developed ownership at the workplace. We had the campus planning teams, long before site-based management ever became popular, of teachers and parents, led by the principal looking at the correlates of school effectiveness and writing a plan for the continuous improvement of that campus."

Guthrie's team — headed by Gary Mathews, who later became the superintendent of St. John's County (Florida) Public School District — tore down the old bureaucratic myopia in the central office as well as in the schools, and realigned policies, procedures, and practices. Guthrie wanted ownership of the change process to be disseminated throughout the system, most importantly, involving teachers, students, and parents. What Guthrie and his team did was dismantle the four elements of bureaucratic management that are familiar to most school districts. Peter Block in *The Empowered Manager* (1987) defines these elements as follows:

> Patriarchal Contract: "top-down, high-control orientation."
> Myopic Self-Interest: "self-interest defined in terms of personal rewards rather than in terms of service and contribution to others."
> Manipulative Tactics: "an autocratic culture and personal ambition conspire to support behavior that is strategic, cautious, and indirect — in other words, manipulative."
> Dependency: "the belief that our survival is in someone else's hands is in part a consequence of the first three parts of the bureaucratic cycle. Our initial willingness to be dependent also helps to create the cycle."

Instead, Guthrie's team shifted to Block's "entrepreneurial cycle":

Entrepreneurial Contract: "based on the belief that the most trustworthy source of authority comes from within the person. The primary task of supervision is to help people trust their own instincts and take responsibility for the success of the business."

Enlightened Self-Interest: "success in terms of contribution and service to customers. What we offer people as rewards are jobs that have meaning, the opportunity to learn and create something special, and the chance to grow in a business through their own efforts."

Authentic Tactics: "If we begin to believe it is our business, then we will feel empowered to act on our own values. For most of us this will mean letting people know where they stand, sharing as much information as possible, sharing control, and taking reasonable risks. . . . It takes courage."

Autonomy: "Autonomy reduces the need for us to give so much attention and power to those above us." We build within ourselves outward with the vision of service to all. (pp. 21-24)

Spring Branch's shared vision has been brought to life in each school, where autonomy, authenticity, and enlightened self-interest are at the heart of the site-based management. The shared decision making allows for ownership of the vision, and that ownership translates into accountability for the achievement of all students.

The entire staff of Spring Branch laid a foundation for a systemic change process by attending many staff development opportunities that were available, including retreats away from the district with colleagues and outside experts.

"My job has always been and continues, even more so, to be one of empowerment and encouragement," says Guthrie. "To permit the system to get out of the way in order that these schools may do what only they know is necessary and right in order to flourish. And if we have learned anything for certain since we began, it is that if people own the project, own the improvement efforts that they're after, then they will make the change process work so student achievement improves for all students."

Another leader in the change process is Judy Stevens, executive director of elementary education. She is responsible for much of the "constructivist" movement by which this Texas district has elevated its employees and students from failure to success and transformed them all into knowledge workers. Scores have gone up on both norm-referenced and criterion-referenced tests. But just as important (and many would say more important) is that Spring Branch is a district where one can see the very latest in curriculum development, instructional techniques, alterations in grading patterns, reporting structures, and scheduling. These changes are bringing new vitality to the schools. There is an interdisciplinary curriculum that exceeds anything being proposed at the teaching colleges, and ownership and pride among faculty and staff — as well as praise from the community — has made Spring Branch a symbol of effective, improving systemic school change.

Adopting Guthrie's successful approach of a year of study preliminary to restructuring, Stevens asked teachers and curriculum coordinators first to examine the latest literature of brain-based learning, authentic assessment, and cross-disciplinary planning. An intensive, voluntary program of staff development followed. And now Stevens and her team of coordinators are leading a revolution in learning and teaching techniques. This revolution is being replicated in school districts throughout the country, growing from the fertile garden of the Effective Schools Improvement Process.

Change in St. John's County, Florida

Gary Mathews was the associate superintendent in Spring Branch during its renewal process, and he also had successfully implemented the Effective Schools Process as the principal of Calloway High School in Jackson, Mississippi. It was only natural that he brought those experiences to bear on his work as superintendent of schools in St. John's County, Florida.

With its northern border touching Jacksonville, St. John's County covers more than 600 square miles, ranging from the picturesque city of St. Augustine — the oldest city in America — to the white beaches of Ponte Verde (home of the PGA), from the drug- and violence-strained neighborhoods of St. Augustine to the poor, untended farmlands of Hastings, once the lettuce and cabbage capital of Florida. The county school district's 19,000 pupils are 84% white, 13% black, and 3% Hispanic, Asian, and American Indian. As in most Florida schools, the proportion of immigrant and disadvantaged pupils is projected to increase.

Until 1992, St. John's County elected its superintendent of schools. The last elected superintendent to this predominantly white, middle-class district was Otis Mason, a black man. Mason is remembered as a superintendent who introduced some participatory leadership. "Otis Mason was a truly lovely man," says Sharon Hartsell, chairwoman of the five-member St. John's school board. "Prior to him, though, it was very top-down, with the superintendents pitting one group against another. So when Otis decided to retire, the board decided it was time to go to the voters and ask them if they wanted to continue this system."

The people of St. John's County voted "overwhelmingly" to go with a superintendent that was to be hired by the school board, rather than elected. When Mathews met with the board for his first interview, a two-hour introduction that was broadcast on the local cable channel, he told them that he was "passionately committed" to Effective Schools and that he had spent his whole career as a data-driven change agent. He talked about the need to bring in all the stakeholders in the operation of the public schools. Without offending his potential constituents, he told them he suspected that much of the teaching pedagogy in St. John's was outmoded and that in order for him to succeed and for student achievement to improve, that pedagogy would have to change.

He emphasized that he would not be working alone, that he would create leaders around him, and that there would be shared decision making, schoolwide planning, and districtwide planning. The board hired Mathews. Before he crossed the threshold of the superintendent's office in downtown St. Augustine, he already was in the early stages of establishing a total of nine strategic planning committees — drawn from the business, social service, academic, and community leadership arenas — to begin work on school improvement.

Although he always has been a believer in bringing in all the constituents, an incident in Spring Branch convinced him, more than ever, that change must have the consensus of the majority of the stakeholders. When the administration of Spring Branch Memorial High School made a move, in the context of detracking, to reduce advanced placement classes, the community erupted in disapproval. Although well into the improvement process, Memorial High was one of Spring Branch's sacred cows; and tampering with advanced placement classes was like getting caught in a field with some angry bulls. Some people say the administration of Memorial High approached the problem all wrong, others that the conservative element in the community was lying in wait for an issue and this became it. For whatever reason, Superintendent Guthrie had to back down at Memorial High on his previously strong stance against tracking.

"I realized at the height of the Memorial High crisis," says Mathews, "that unless you explain the change and get the buy-in from the various stakeholder groups all the way up to the school board, and certainly with respect to the community in which the school resides, the change is going to be short-lived at best." Without the buy-in, says Mathews, a school ends up under siege; and no one learns in a school under siege. Plus, it puts the entire improvement process in jeopardy.

Mathews is not going to make that mistake. He says he will not allow any of the schools in St. John's to come "under siege," that he will see to it that each school improvement team works with a consensus, and that before any issue with the potential of dividing the community even rears its head, he will make certain there is an information system in place. This system will provide the stakeholder groups with research data and other information.

But first must come what Mathews refers to as the most important tenet of school improvement: the moral imperative that characterizes Effective Schools. "There is still no doubt that the first thing one has to commit to is some sense of morality about what schools are charged to do. That sense of morality has to do with teaching in the public sector anyone who comes through the door," says Mathews. "Once you have that, then you build the critical mass of support around that belief system. And that critical mass must be data-driven, research-based, committed to the moral imperative of teaching for learning for all."

In September of 1992, just one month after he arrived, Mathews held a workshop in one of the middle schools, where he stated that there would be no compromising on the need for radical change in the district schools. He was opening up the governing process, transforming it from closed management to open collaboration. He brought all the stakeholder groups of that particular middle school (a school that served a cross-section of St. John's students) and explained the characteristics of Effective Schools. Mathews, who uses "heading west" as a metaphor for the cultural and leadership change he is seeking, says that the people in the county were not only ready for change, they were willing to make the necessary sacrifices in order for that change to be done right. Leadership, says Mathews, is to "get the herd to head roughly west."

The first thing was to help the stakeholders understand the Effective Schools Process. "I spent a lot of time modeling the [planning process], which is what the people needed," explains Mathews. "I modeled, discussed, and defined the critical attributes of school improvement plans." Part of the ongoing inservice program included taking apart another plan from another system (Spring Branch) and evaluating that plan so that everyone could understand what the critical issues were in a successful plan that was actually implemented elsewhere.

Needs assessment also was ongoing in every school. Following extensive inservice, Mathews gave the schools a great deal of latitude in the needs assessment process, a decision he says has been the most empowering for the individuals and teams in the schools.

Also essential to Mathew's restructuring agenda is empowerment of principals as collaborators in reform. Good instructional leaders take their leadership from many quarters, says Mathews, not just the faculty. They look to the custodians, the secretarial staff, parents, and neighbors. Indeed, in our book, *Keepers of the Dream* (1994), we state that the active involvement of everyone from bus drivers to the managers of local apartment complexes is essential to the leadership of successful principals.

Mathews maintains, "It is kind of thinking outside the box a little bit and saying, hey, unless you give the community understanding in buying into some change, the school staff, and the team — which is working, ideally, daily with the principal — unless you get those stakeholder groups buying in — and remember this includes the school board — then a) it probably is not going to succeed, and b) you could potentially end up under siege by any or all of these stakeholders."

Mathews offers two examples of where his consensus formula has operated as he expected. At one point, the school board was considering inviting a conservative, pro-abstinence speaker on sex education for a school assembly. Mathews asked the various stakeholder groups for their opinions; and when the board took a vote of 3 to 2, Mathews raised the question of consensus. Consensus clearly had not been achieved, and so the issue died.

The question of consensus rose again when the Mill Creek Elementary School wanted to become a "full-service" school by bringing in community health services for its students, including social programs and mental health services. Conservative members of the community objected.

"Oh, we had a major rhubarb over that one," recalls school board head Sharon Hartsell. "Members of the community started saying we were getting into areas we didn't belong, that by bringing in mental health services we were serving people other than the immediate school population. There was a major fight as they charged we'd have all these weirdoes wandering around the campus."

While Mathews and the board stood back and watched and listened to the constituents, the principal and the school improvement team took a chapter out of Mathews' consensus book and applied what they had learned. Says Hartsell, "The principal let the school improvement team explain to all the stakeholders why it was important for Mill Creek to be full-service and why it would help everyone in the community. They went out and educated the community."

By the time Mill Creek began implementing its full-service programs, the "major rhubarb" at Mill Creek was long gone. The stakeholders were in full support. "This is the first time this district has seen any real collaboration," says Hartsell, who has been involved for two decades with the St. John's schools and also serves on the state's school improvement team. "There's no doubt in my mind, and I think most board members' minds, that this is working for us and for the schools. Collaboration is for real, and the schools are starting to believe it."

Mathews explains that a long-range strategic plan must be developed in such a way that:

- It honors the past but looks to the future.
- It solicits involvement of all stakeholders.
- It scans external and internal environments for relevant data and research findings.

By adhering to these three principles, the plan can ensure that:

- District beliefs, mission, and vision are established or reaffirmed.
- Goals and objectives are clear and achievable.

- Work in schools is high quality and "consumer oriented."
- Collaborative leadership is standard operating procedure.
- School processes support ongoing analysis of effectiveness.
- Accountability is fostered through formative and summative evaluation.

Mathews also believes that stakeholder roles must change in order for collaboration and consensus management to work. Parents:

- must shift from "What's good for my child?" to "What's good for all children?"
- must be guided away from rivalries and factions that divide stakeholders in schools; and
- must work with nonparent constituents on site-based committees and be open to new partnerships.

Teachers:
- must have time to teach;
- must become adept in group dynamics and in building consensus with parents and administrators;
- must be well-informed and alert to issues affecting all schools;
- must become familiar with research on school improvement; and
- must become risk-takers.

Principals:
- must be allowed authority and freedom to use it independent of the central office;
- must defend decisions on merit and consensus, rather than simply policy;
- must be directly accountable for processes, whether they succeed or fail;
- must have sharp human relations skills and be adept at group dynamics;
- must accurately analyze community needs;
- must create new relationships with constituents; and
- must find ways to empower all staff members.

To accomplish these changes, Mathews also has included in the St. John's strategic plan a detailed outline of the roles and tasks of the superintendent, the school board, and central office administrators. Explains Mathews, "We started out with the purpose of creating a school system for the 21st century that would teach for learning for all. That's what we are after. To have all of our students, all of our people, in a healthy, lifelong-learning environment. We have begun a long-term improvement process toward our vision."

Transformations in Springfield, Massachusetts

In 1989, Springfield, Massachusetts, Superintendent Peter Negroni began a reform process that, according to him, is moving along on schedule. "We are hardly done, but we have a strong beginning," he wrote in *The State of the Nation's Public Schools* (1993).

There is some political unrest in Springfield from those who question the long-range plan and do not understand why the learning gap between socioeconomic groups cannot be lessened more rapidly. But, in general, people believe that the Springfield Public Schools are moving in the right direction. The fact that the 40 Springfield schools are "moving" at all is noteworthy, not merely because this formerly heavily industrialized city has a school population that is two-thirds minority and one-half in poverty, but also because Springfield is operating under a state court-ordered desegregation plan.

Between desegregation, shifting populations, local politics, and an increasingly conservative Massachusetts legislature, Negroni, like other reform-minded leaders, faces an uphill battle. He knows that in order to win this fight, or even to stay on a level field with the opposition, he, too, has to pull in segments of the entire community. To do so, he launched a campaign not just to cooperate with the media, but to become a partner with newspapers, radio, and television stations. He needed more than air time and print space. He needed their support.

What Negroni, Mathews, Guthrie, and most superintendents walking the plank of renewal realize is that one cannot succeed without public communications strategies. Negroni formed a marketing committee of media representatives and school employees. Through them, he has created advocates for his reform in the press. There were special newspaper and television campaigns, articles and programs designed to inform all residents. Viewers have been barraged with public service announcements, billboards, and bus ads, and local companies have donated space. The message is: "If You Love Learning, So Will Your Children."

Similar to the strategic plans drawn up by Guthrie and Mathews, the Negroni team's "Blueprint for Excellence" set out the district mission and vision and the guidelines for implementation of school-based management. The school-based management teams began work in 1989, the first year of Negroni's reform. By 1991, the school-based decision-making process had been incorporated into the teachers' contract.

Effective Schools tenets are woven into the Springfield reforms. "One cannot have an effective quality of life in any community without effective public schools," writes Negroni. "Equity is the single most critical issue in education today." Answering the call to equity, Negroni believes, must be coupled with a recognition of future employment realities. Those realities, contends Negroni, are "moving us from a moral imperative to educate all to an economic imperative to educate all." He cites figures showing that 16 million new jobs will be created by American industry by the beginning of the 21st century, but there will be only 14 million people to fill those jobs. Not only will the nation be short two million workers, but many of those 14 million workers, the majority of whom will be female or minority, will lack the necessary skills to succeed unless today's education is reformed to more effectively meet their needs (Negroni 1993).

In order to rebuild the Springfield schools and teach all children, Negroni believes that the system must go through a complete metamorphosis, which he breaks down into four essential transformations: organizational, pedagogical, social and attitudinal, and political.

In the organizational transformation, Negroni's staff is examining, among other standard procedures, the tracking system, Carnegie units, the retention policy, the present 6-hour school day, age-grade grouping, and staff development. Some changes have been initiated. Time has been scheduled for teachers to plan and work on professional development, and the school day is no longer locked into six hours. Scheduling and use of time in general are being analyzed.

In the area of pedagogical transformation, Negroni and his staff have examined the changes in instructional strategies that mark progressive public school districts and the most highly regarded private schools — the physiological evidence on how learning takes place in the human brain. Negroni states flatly, "Teachers must recognize that the skills and information they brought to teaching are no longer adequate." Thus he has implemented extensive new training and staff development support for the Springfield teachers.

Change in beliefs are at the heart of Springfield's social and attitudinal transformation. Using business leaders, community people, and the media, Negroni is hoping to put as much pressure on his district from the outside as he is from the inside. Through speeches, community gatherings, meetings with heads of business and industry, Negroni discusses the changing economic needs of the nation and western Massachusetts. His message is one of inclusion, diversity, and multiculturalism. He talks about a future where "what we do in schools with children who come to school will make the difference" between prosperity and despair.

But the most difficult task is political transformation. Negroni writes:

> Does the country have the will to educate those who traditionally have been ignored? Will American society understand the political and economic repercussions and implications of not educating its poor? Will American soci-

ety support public education in urban centers when the people being educated do not resemble both in class and color the people controlling the economy in those urban centers? (1993, p. 157)

Political transformation, Negroni insists, must involve consideration of the present inequities in school funding, as well as the financial and social problems inherent in many school choice plans. Springfield has a "controlled" school choice plan that allows parents to choose within a specific education zone or from citywide magnet schools. This plan has met with success, but a state-adopted school choice plan causes concern for education planners.

In order for these four transformations to take place, Negroni writes that 15 "precepts" must be accepted, including: everyone must be educated, even if it costs more; current funding is inequitable; the current education model must be reformed; curriculum must be changed to reflect goals for the 21st century; what does not work must be recognized and abandoned; ongoing staff development is essential; teachers need more time to work and plan; and schools must meet community needs.

Springfield has a long way to go in its reform, but the district merits watching. Negroni has built his reform around the new literature of collaborative leadership, the financial realities of his district, and a quarter-century of Effective Schools Research. Like many superintendents, he has bolstered his district's organization using the Effective Schools Process. Now, as he pushes into the realms of cognitive psychology, constructivist teaching, and other pedagogical reforms, he brings the latest in staff development to his district. As the struggle for transformation moves forward, its beginnings in the belief that all children can learn — and must learn — are evident.

20 Years of Effective Schools in Arizona

In the early 1970s, the conference site was the Tacky Bird Ranch outside Tucson. Gerry George was an assistant principal from the Glendale Union High School District. George remembers that the "in-thing" at the education conference was "accountability." Although much of the conference focused on Chapter 1, George recalls that three questions were posed that imprinted onto his psyche and over time became vital to his leadership in the implementation of the Effective Schools Process:

- What do your many publics desire in terms of learner performance?
- How effective is the district in bringing about the desired learner performance?
- If you are not as effective as desired, what are you going to do about it?

"The words and catch phrases are always changing in this business," says Gerry George, superintendent of the 13,000-student, nine-high school district that includes parts of Phoenix and neighboring Glendale. "But what works does not change. In this district, consensus with the Effective Schools correlates has always been the right formula."

The school district boasts the highest math and language arts scores in the state of Arizona. Students score in the top 15% nationwide in the college entrance exams. The high schools have some of the lowest dropout rates in the country. George, who has been superintendent for more than 12 years, says there is one reason for Glendale's success today: Effective Schools.

"Without Effective Schools, we would be down the tubes, no question," says George. "Sure, our teachers would still be working their hearts out, don't get me wrong. But they would not be sensitized, they would not have the tools, the skills; and the leadership, at the district and school levels, just wouldn't be there."

Nor would they have the support of the community. Back in the 1970s when George and other administrators went looking for the answers to those three questions, they began a process that in the 1990s has become routine for most improving districts. They went to the newspapers, television and radio stations, public officials, community leaders, and the staffs of the schools and asked, "What do you want out of the schools?" In the 1970s, the question was almost revolutionary.

It took a year to ask the question and organize the responses. What came back, says George, essentially mirrored the "Cardinal Principles" of 1917. Everyone wants students to learn math, science, writing, reading, communication skills, and a little citizenship. Over the next two decades these "desires" of the public would never change, though they would be re-evaluated and the curriculum would be retooled every 5 to 7 years in Glendale. Now, for example, instead of "goals," educators refer to "exit-out codes" or "exit outcomes." But the essentials have remained constant.

Over the years, Glendale and Gerry George have been able to avoid controversies that have led to siege conditions in other districts, because everything the school district has done has included the different Glendale constituencies. "Schools are effective to the extent that they produce results which satisfy all the constituencies that must be satisfied in order to maintain the commitments and resources needed to sustain the school in the pursuit of its purpose," explains George.

The natural place to take the discussion of results was to the teachers, which George, then director of curriculum, did. Beginning 20 years ago, the district started to ask the teachers to assess their learning environments, in particular the curriculum, and to answer the second question: How effective is the district in bringing about the desired learning performance?

"It was simply, here's what the community wants, what are you giving them? And if it's not what they want, then how do we change in order to give them what they want? It was the teachers and department chairs telling us what was required in order to get the results," says George.

By 1982, Gerry George was superintendent of the Glendale schools, scores were going up, accountability was still the watchword of the day, but, says George, "We were missing something, something very important."

The issue was testing. People were comparing schools based on the tests; and without mission statements, a belief system, or an overall process to be followed, there was no cohesiveness. Or as George puts it, "I was fighting the test thing from one end of the district to the other. Depending upon where the schools sat, it was either feast or famine. It was a real bloodletting. Without the process and the correlates, it was one crisis after another. No unity."

George returned to the Effective Schools Research, immersed himself in the emerging data and new applications, and decided that this was the one process that was not only "the right thing to do," but the systemic process that would work in Glendale. He once again went to the constituents and put together a districtwide steering committee that created a definition of school effectiveness for the Glendale Union District:

> An effective school in the Glendale Union High School District is one which assures 1) measurable academic achievement and 2) observable growth in emotional maturity, physical well-being, and social responsibility by all students.

As important as this definition, and the mandate that all nine high schools become Effective Schools, were Glendale's accompanying "eight characteristics" of school effectiveness. While the Effective Schools research was in its early growth, and Edmonds was emphasizing just five correlates, Glendale's districtwide committee pushed further; and the faculty representatives of each school developed a specific set of indicators for their eight characteristics:

Clear and specific school purpose
- clearly stated
- used in decision making
- understood by students, staff, and parents

Strong educational leadership by administrators
- visible and accessible

- responsible to faculty and students
- responsive to parents/community
- provide instructional leadership
- maintain NCA approved pupil/teacher ratio

High expectations of students and staff
- believe that all students can learn
- stress academic achievement
- see teachers as most important to achievement

School partnership with parents and community
- communicate positively with parents
- maintain parental support network
- parents share responsibility for discipline and achievement, attend school events

Positive climate for learning
- school is neat, clean, physically safe
- characterized by pervasive caring
- rewards/praises academic achievement
- reinforces positive student behavior
- students adhere to school rules
- display high time on task

Frequent monitoring of student progress
- appropriate assignments and practice
- prompt feedback for performance
- optimal classroom participation
- multiple assessments

Emphasis on student attainment of essential skills
- students accountable for reading, writing, computing, spelling in all classes; receive instruction in essential skills
- administration shows high commitment to the teaching of essential skills

- teachers receive adequate materials for teaching essential skills

High level of faculty commitment
- teachers help students before, during, after school
- teachers help formulate school improvement goals
- staff enforces district and school policies
- staff exhibits professional conduct and attire

Designing the descriptive standards for the correlates, or characteristics, took time and energy. But it was time and energy — and money — that George was more than willing to spend. "I knew that school effectiveness was the model we needed. But I also knew I didn't have the time to single-handedly bring the process in."

George hired C.M. "Mac" Bernd (later the superintendent of California's San Marcos School District and subsequently the Newport Beach District) and dubbed him "Administrator of Effective Schools." Bernd became better known throughout the district as "Mr. Effective Schools." Bernd set up School Effectiveness Teams (SET) in each high school and a districtwide Super SET. The process model that the teams came up with took three years to develop.

Bringing in, or recruiting someone from the staff, to work exclusively on the change process with the schools is a tactic being espoused by many reformers today. But it was not a common procedure at that time.

"It all fit together perfectly," says George, "except for one major failing. And it wasn't Mac's fault, because at that time he didn't have the training; but what we did not learn at that time was the whole process of interweaving consensus building, problem solving, and pyramid decision making." This became the next struggle for Glendale as they brought together accountability with school-based decision making.

George recounts an incident that happened after Bernd left the district in the mid-1980s. "I'm over with one of the SET teams," began George, "and they're talking about how, in the women's bathroom, if you reach over to dry your hands, you get water on a bench, and something should be done about that. I was stunned. This is not what the teams are supposed to be about. This is not school effectiveness. And the teachers were as upset as I was."

What George was going through in the mid-1980s was what many school districts working with the Effective Schools Process were discovering: The weak link was the principal-as-sole-leader model. Teachers and principals alike needed the shared decision-making skills. Since that time, the National Center for Effective Schools has created leadership and decision-making programs and training modules that are being used throughout the country. But ten years ago, the research and data were just beginning to build. Superintendents like Gerry George had to look elsewhere. George contracted collaborative leadership consultants and hired one person to work half time as a trainer. Every school brought in a teacher, a principal, a staff member (such as a secretary or custodian), a parent, and a student and taught them to be trainers for their schools.

George and the Glendale administrators discovered what is accepted knowledge today in Effective Schools districts: Staff development — particularly in instructional leadership, shared decision making, and school-based management — must be available to the entire school community. It is not sufficient to train just a few key people.

"We continue to do a considerable amount of staff development in all areas, especially leadership training and collaborative skills," says George. "We know how essential it is. If a teacher wants to know more about expectations, it's available. If they want to know more about how to collaboratively operate a school, that's there." The schools, through their own planning teams, can set up any additional staff development they deem necessary for the enhancement of their particular community.

Each year, hundreds of educators travel to the Glendale Union High School District to examine what appears to be one of the longest running Effective Schools Processes in the country. The commitment of teachers and staff to quality and equity does not vary, although the individual school procedures differ from one another. Teams still operate on each campus, though at least one high school, Glendale High School, has had some recent trouble with maintaining teacher involvement. George notes that the school has experienced considerable administrator turnover in the last several years, but is now under "solid, new leadership." Whatever Glendale High's present problems with the faculty serving on teams, they have not affected students' achievement scores, which remain high. The school's equity index also notes little difference in the achievement levels of students on the basis of parent education levels.

"There will always be the highs and lows within any school district," says George. "But with the Effective Schools Process, we know what we are supposed to be doing and what we are doing. We also are able to look to the future and plan our students and staff for that future."

Conclusion

The four superintendents featured in this chapter employ very different leadership styles. Spring Branch's Hal Guthrie is a leader who says: "I'll give you the details of what I want in a building. How you construct it and get the desired results is up to you." St. John's County's Gary Mathews is a leader who is moving out into the community, bringing in all the stakeholders for their input into communitywide renewal of schools. Springfield's Peter Negroni is working for a turn-around, taking on the political and pedagogical opponents by working as much "from the outside as from the inside." And Glendale's Gerry George has spent years balancing political whims, legislative mandates, and local egos by working on doing "all the right things" using a carefully designed rubric of community involvement and outside expertise.

However, the thing that drives all of these superintendents is the moral imperative that all children will learn the intended curricula. Each maneuvers within the political arena, bending to the forces around him and juggling mandates, desires, and responsibilities. But by using consensus about the Effective Schools correlates and the Effective Schools Process, each of these superintendents also is building lasting reform.

The key, of course, is accountability. They achieve the desired results. Their personal styles and means of implementation vary; their ends never do. Such is the compelling power of Effective Schools.

Chapter 7

Facing the Future: How Effective Schools Meet the Challenges

Should we look to the future with hope or despair? Alfred North Whitehead, in his 1929 book, *Aims of Education and Other Essays*, wrote:

> When one considers in its length and breadth, the impor-
> tance of the nation's young, the broken lives, the defeated
> hopes, the national failures, which result from the frivolous
> inertia with which [education] is treated, it is difficult to
> restrain within oneself a savage rage.

Toni Morrison, in *The Bluest Eye* (1994), echoes Whitehead's sentiment when she describes Pecola's story: "A little black girl yearns for the blue eyes of a little white girl, and the horror at the heart of her yearning is exceeded only by the evil of fulfillment" (p. 204).

America's Religious Right does not approve of many of the writings of Nobel Prize winning novelist Toni Morrison. In many communities, parents who follow the tenets of the social conservatism that has become increasingly strident in public education have been successful in pulling Morrison's books from the shelves of school libraries.

One of Morrison's books that incites conservative ire is *The Bluest Eye*. It is the story of a young black girl, Pecola, who lives in poverty of home, community, and spirit. She believes she is ugly, of no value, and that only by having blue eyes will someone think she is of worth and believe in her and her dreams. Her life, her spirit, is bruised. And after she is raped, she goes mad, believing that she finally has the precious blue eyes. The neighbors and her false friends abandon her to exist alone in her fantasy. Morrison concludes:

> All of us — all who knew her — felt so wholesome after we cleaned ourselves on her. . . . And she let us, and thereby deserved our contempt. We honed our egos on her, padded our characters with her frailty, and yawned in the fantasy of our strength. (p. 205)

The classrooms of too many American public schools are wastelands for children like Pecola. They are places of fear and punitive assessment, where children yearn for someone to believe in them. Instead, the children become victims all over again, victims of those who should protect them and who, instead, bolster their own egos and pad their own perceived well-being through the pain of these children and their families.

This is a harsh, but true statement. One has only to look at the conditions in America's inner-city schools, at the spirits of many of the students inside those schools, and at their lives outside the schools. We know their future — unless we work to change it.

In the fall of 1994, the Washington, D.C., public schools, whose students are 92% black, did not open on schedule because of "life-threatening" fire-code violations. More than 20 schools were unsafe. Many had not been inspected in 30 years. Parents had fought for years to have the fire code enforced and had received little, if any, response. Finally, they filed a class-action lawsuit. A court ordered the school department that June to fix the violations. In September, the schools were still in violation.

Would this situation have happened in a white, affluent suburb such as Westchester? The answer is no.

Over the years the schools of our nation's capital have spent millions on consultants, gurus, and "flavor-of-the-month" panaceas to solve their education problems. School officials, who complain about not having the money to repair fire-code violations, say they do not have an exact figure but admit that millions have been spent on "outside consultants." Teachers and principals add confirmation. But what do the city schools have to show for all their outside help? According to the *Washington Post* of 18 and 19 January 1995:

- A dropout rate of almost 50%.
- Achievement scores almost one-third below other cities.
- Students and teachers shot in several schools.

The percentage of families living below the poverty level has almost tripled since the 1970s. In 1993-94, the proportion of Washington residents living below the poverty level jumped from 20% to 26%, and the number receiving food stamps grew from 77,000 to 98,000.

Although Washington, D.C., is an extreme situation, it is hardly unique. When New York City released its reading and math scores in July 1994 — scores that for the first time had been disaggregated by race and ethnicity — no one was really surprised that there was a learning gap between the poorer and the more well-to-do districts and schools. People were surprised only that the gap was so great. According to the *New York Times* of 8 July 1994:

- In reading, 43% of black students and 37% of Hispanic students scored at or above grade level, compared to 65% of Asian and Pacific Islanders and 70% of non-Hispanic whites.
- In math, 41% of black students and 43% of Hispanic students were at or above grade level, while 77% of Asian and Pacific Islanders and 74% of whites were at or above grade level.

Although school officials pointed out that some majority-black schools produced high scores on the tests, most of the low scores came from the poor and disadvantaged neighborhoods.

The tragedy is not that these disparities exist. Rather, the tragedy is that we know how to fix ineffective schools and yet have not done so.

The Danger of the Bell Curve

American education suffers from a "bell curve" mentality that posits a distribution of talent and achievement in which some students must always fall at the low end. Thus, the argument goes, if failure for some is inevitable, why bother with the low end?

For too many Americans, this kind of thinking means that the answer to education's problems is not to solve them and improve schools, but to blame students and parents — and teachers and administrators — for their supposed shortcomings. Doing so allows the critics to offer biased, illegitimate, and wrong-headed "solutions" that further endanger our schools and our children.

A recent example of this fundamental wrong-headedness can be found in Charles Murray and Richard Herrnstein's book, *The Bell Curve* (1994). In this book, the authors would have us believe that the reason blacks score lower on standardized tests is because African Americans are genetically inferior and that their intellect and reasoning ability are less than that of Caucasian, Asian, and Jewish peoples.

The statistics and conclusions reached by these authors have been criticized by social scientists and statisticians as deeply flawed. But the damage was done as soon as the first publicity release appeared. That first impression cannot easily be erased from the public's mind — especially because such prejudice, which is eagerly fed by the rhetoric of the Religious Right, is held by a substantial minority in the United States.

The message of *The Bell Curve* is that America would be better off halting reform efforts for the disadvantaged because those students are genetically inferior and the reform efforts won't work. The best use of education monies would be to concentrate on the middle and upper classes, the "cognitive elite."

We've heard this cry before. *The Bell Curve* authors contend that we should stop spending money on the disadvantaged because schools cannot make a difference in the intellectual growth of black students — and any progress that has been made is the result of "dumbing down" the curriculum. At one point the authors attack inner-city programs, specifically citing Marva Collins' work, stating that there is no proof of success, or growth, for the students within these schools. This is just not true. There are test results, graduation figures, and statistics on students who go on to college that prove the effectiveness of such exemplary inner-city programs.

The Bell Curve authors also assert that their "findings" of intellectual inferiority should make no difference in the day-to-day life and interactions of blacks and whites. That is perhaps the most outrageous statement of all. In a recent classroom analysis, black students in a Maryland public school revealed that they believe their race is dumber, less motivated, and more prone to violence and neglect than other races. This stereotype, erected over the past 270 years, is believed by the very children who today suffer from its malicious effects. Yet, collectively, educators have done little to move forward; and many critics of education would have us move backward. This will not do for the future.

Indeed, there is increasing pressure on schools from conservative and religious fundamentalist communities to revert to "the ways schools used to be." Teachers and administrators are legitimately afraid of the growing power of the Religious Right. That movement's effects cannot be ignored. Religious Right politicians, including school board candidates, espouse a variety of "reforms," including: teaching creationism, opposing full-service schools and school-based health clinics; discontinuing Head Start programs; rejecting federal dollars for breakfast programs; banning textbooks and library books that are "too liberal"; firing gay and lesbian teachers; dismantling multicultural education programs; and doing away with drug and alcohol abuse prevention programs — to name but a few.

In Virginia, which refused federal funds that the governor said would lead to further government interference, the sex education programs that once gave students vital information about the prevention of AIDS and other sexually transmitted diseases have been discontinued. In many Pennsylvania communities, outcome-

109

based education has been tossed out with accusations that it teaches "affective education" that emphasizes "secular humanism."

The various groups that make up the Religious Right, from Concerned Women of America to the Christian Coalition, are well-funded, powerful, and expanding. What *The Bell Curve* and the 1994 midterm elections that brought a conservative majority to Congress are about is the heart of Effective Schools: expectations. In the past — that status quo, "the way things used to be" — we did not believe in all children. If we do not believe that all children can learn, then they won't. Period.

We have seen the difference that believing in children can make. We have proof of that difference. And now, using the Effective Schools Process, we are in the midst of a pedagogical shift at the instructional and leadership levels that can make profound achievement a reality for all students. We must not step back.

We know, as the statistics of poverty and ignorance in the inner-cities proclaim, that we have already failed generations of school children. In the future we must bring in the generations we failed — the parents and grandparents of the children — and make them part of the community learning process in order for education to move beyond the school walls. We must have high expectations for all and passionately accept that all will learn if given time and opportunity. We have the data. We have had them for a quarter-century. The data prove that those expectations are ladders to achievement. We must embrace and institutionalize the lessons of Effective Schools.

The fact is that in communities as diverse as Spencerport, New York; District 6 in Spanish Harlem; Glendale, Arizona; Spring Branch, Texas; Frederick County, Maryland; and many others, proof can be found in achievement scores, teacher morale, budgetary and personnel restructuring and accountability, and increased involvement from stakeholders throughout the community that the Effective Schools Process is real, viable, and enduring.

Historian and philosopher Alfred North Whitehead spoke of "the broken lives, the defeated hopes, the national failures, which result from the frivolous inertia" that marked society's dealings with public education in the 1920s. Today, teachers and staff still struggle in the rubble of neglected schools. We ask the metaphorical question that *A Nation at Risk* asked: If a foreign power came into our country and each year destroyed thousands of young children, would we not mount a war to defeat this enemy?

The enemy is us.

Toward a New Stewardship

There is enough progress being made in inner-city Effective Schools to believe that the education establishment is ready to stop blaming the child, to stop catering to the consultants and gurus and special interests, and to make the leadership and instructional changes necessary to teach all children.

Despite the rhetoric of intolerance heard in the political arena, the indifference that was destroying our public education system and the lives within it gradually is being replaced by a realization that if we are to save our democracy, our American way of life, then we must first save our public schools. While sociologists will argue whether we are doing this for humanitarian reasons or economic reasons, those who care about all children are just glad some leaders are finally taking action. It has taken anger and violence and the looming fact that 36% of our school population will be students from minority backgrounds by the year 2000. But, at last, change seems to lie ahead.

Peter Block's recent book, *Stewardship* (1993) is a worthy touchstone that is finding its way onto the desks of busy teachers and principals. Block, who wrote the 1987 bestseller, *The Empowered Manager*, concentrates on the virtue of choosing service over self-interest. He emphasizes "reconciliation," the principle that if we live and conduct business in a way that guarantees the prosperity of the future for the next generation, then we will achieve a self-fulfillment that is otherwise unattainable. Writes Block in *Stewardship*:

Stewardship begins with the willingness to be account-able for some larger body than ourselves: an organization, a community. Stewardship springs from a set of beliefs about reforming organizations that affirms our choice for service over the pursuit of self-interest. When we choose service over self-interest we say we are willing to be deeply account-able without choosing to control the world around us. It requires a level of trust that we are not used to holding. (p. 6)

In Effective Schools, there is a reawakening of this sense of stewardship. It is not the romantic, barefoot idealism of the 1960s, but rather an informed understanding that we must take action to save our schools and the children in them.

"You see in the schools not only people you never saw before, never expected to see," says Melba Vallas, principal of Moon Valley High School in Glendale, Arizona, "but you also see a concentrated effort on the part of parents who now believe their input truly matters." Vallas continues: "These are all the stake-holders, and I involve every one of them. When I have a problem with a kid and drugs, there are doctors closely involved with this school I can privately seek help from. And if I need good, basic advice, well, there's a lady who works in our cafeteria that is one of the most important people in this school. I depend on these stakeholders. They are stewards of these children just as much as I am." This stewardship approach is closely aligned to the Effective Schools Process. Effective Schools build from within and expand outward to draw in their affected communities.

Effective Schools across the country and worldwide (now in more than 30 countries) are countering the cynics' and critics' claims that the disadvantaged cannot be helped. Block points out in *Stewardship* that cynics can be divided into two groups: the victims and the bystanders. The victims believe in hierarchy rather than partnership. They do not want to be held accountable, but they love to complain about having no real power. The bystanders never commit and always refer to any change as an "experiment." In their apathy, they create roadblocks for those who are trying to create change. The ranks of education — as well as its critics — are filled with victims and bystanders. According to Block, the best way to defeat them is to include them in what he calls the freedom, the service, the adventure of change.

Teachers themselves are among the most cynical; and administrators often foster cynicism by dividing the faculty, setting up cliques for control, and refusing to take actions that might raise teachers' spirits. Cynical administrators are products of a professional education system that tends to protect the status quo, which in turn produces more cynics.

Noted educator John Goodlad holds back no punches in his assessment that we will not see the growth of good schools without good teacher education programs. But in his recent book, *Educational Renewal* (1994), he believes that there is room for hope in the growing realization of the interconnectedness of good teaching programs and good schools. This is a change from the story he told in his 1990 book, *Teachers for Our Nation's Schools*. In that book he wrote, "A young education professor looked at me in disbelief when I asked him about his involvements with schools: 'The problems of the schools are no concern of mine,' he said" (p. 67).

In *Educational Renewal*, Goodlad notes that John Dewey called for a department of pedagogy at the University of Chicago in a letter to the Board of Trustees in 1896. Goodlad thus renews his earlier call for that center of learning that will focus not only on subject knowledge and instructional theories, but also on "the moral perspective that teaching in schools requires." He calls for a continuous inquiry into the art and science of teaching, an inquiry that will do what medicine did in the early 20th century — bring together the training doctors with the patients, the training teachers with the actual students. But this idea, though far from revolutionary, still frightens many; and that, as he writes in *Educational Renewal*, confounds Goodlad:

> What I find to be particularly puzzling and disturbing
> stems from the tranquillity of the higher education commu-

nity regarding teacher education, especially at a time when universities are coming under sharp criticism for their aloofness from elementary and secondary education and school reform. . . . There is something unreal about this suicidal denial. (pp. 27-28)

However, Goodlad sees hope for bringing the two disparate groups together. First is the momentum for school reform and the fact that the education of educators is finally being tied to that reform. Second is the desire within and outside academia, by at least a few leaders, to improve teacher training. And third is the push by state legislators to hold the state colleges accountable for the millions of dollars they consume annually in their alleged pursuit of quality teacher education. Perhaps most important, Goodlad takes school reform and renewal out of the future and puts it in the present.

Reform in the present tense is at the heart of Peter Negroni's transformations, which were summarized in Chapter 6. Renewal must take place through four essential transformations: organizational, pedagogical, social and attitudinal, and political. Negroni asks: Does every child in America have equal access to an effective and appropriate education? Does the nation have the will to educate those who traditionally have been ignored?

Negroni asks some tough questions, and he poses the tough solution: The education of all children, the revitalization of the teaching process for all teachers, and the involvement of the entire community in the teaching for learning for all.

In closing, we go back to Judy Stevens, the elementary education director in Spring Branch, Texas, whom we introduced in Chapter 1. "If we ignore these children now, if we fail them now, they don't just go to Mars," says Stevens. "All those kids who feel horrible when they leave us and don't think they're worth a dime, they don't disappear. It's a system. They don't leave us. They come right back around the systemic loop and they sort of give us negative feedback, like we pay for them in prisons. We pay for them on welfare. They hold us up in dark alleys. They make life painful for us."

Stevens has seen that, through the Effective Schools Process and its empowerment of teachers and administrators, changes are made in instructional strategies and curricula that catch those children in that systemic loop and serve them, rather than fail them. Through the brain-based learning styles instituted in Spring Branch and other locations and through accompanying curriculum changes, teachers and students are rediscovering learning and fulfillment.

In Effective Schools teachers talk of being both contributor and participant. They realize that John Dewey was right 100 years ago. Dewey said that learning, to be valued by the student, could not be a jumble of disembodied information. Rather, learning must be a patterning of knowledge that involves the whole child and his or her environment and experiences. Now, through extensive teacher training, teachers are being given the tools, the expertise, and the confidence to genuinely teach. There are no excuses anymore.

There is an energy that surges through the observer in schools like those in Spring Branch. It fills one with admiration for the diligent, inspiring students; humility for the commitment and devotion of the teachers; and respect for the integrity and credibility of the principals and the leaders of the district who create the environment for these overwhelmingly successful 21st century schools.

And it is credibility that public education in the 1990s will come back to, must come back to and depend on if it is to survive. Years ago the word *credible* was used to describe what Edmonds and his colleagues were saying. The problem was that the nation was not interested in his credible data, his growing body of credible research. Now we know that Edmonds' credibility has become the truth. The truth is that all children *can* learn, and the credibility of Effective Schools and its improvement process can be the transforming agent for public education.

References

Austin, G.R. "An Analysis of Outlier Exemplary Schools and their Distinguishing Characteristics." Paper presented at the meeting of the American Educational Research Association, San Francisco, April 1979.

Block, Peter. *The Empowered Manager*. San Francisco: Jossey-Bass, 1987.

Block, Peter. *Stewardship*. San Francisco: Barrett-Koehler, 1993.

Brookover, Wilbur. "A Social-Psychological Conception of Classroom Learning." *School and Society* 87 (28 February 1959): 84-87.

Brookover, Wilbur. *School, Classroom Climate, and Classroom Behavior*. East Lansing: Michigan State University, 1983.

Brookover, Wilbur, and Erickson, Edsel. *Society, Schools, and Learning*. Boston: Allyn and Bacon, 1969.

Brookover, Wilbur; Gigliotti, Richard; Henderson, Ronald; and Schneider, Jeffrey. "Elementary School Social Environment and School Achievement." Manuscript. College of Urban Development, Michigan State University, East Lansing, 1973.

Brookover, W.B., and Lezotte, L.W. *Changes in School Characteristics Coincident with Changes in Student Achievement*. (Executive summary). East Lansing: Michigan State University, Institute for Research on Teaching, 1977.

Brookover, W.B.; Paterson, Ann; and Thomas, Shailer. *Self-Concept of Ability and School Achievement*. East Lansing: Michigan State University, Bureau of Research and Publications, 1962.

Brookover, Wilbur; Schweitzer, John; Schneider, Jeffrey; Beady, Charles; Flood, Patricia; and Wisenbaker, Joseph. "School Social Systems and Student Achievement." National Institute of Education (Grant number NIE-G-74-0020), 1979.

Bullard, Pamela, and Taylor, Barbara O. *Making School Reform Happen*. New York: Allyn and Bacon, 1993.

Bullard, Pamela, and Taylor, Barbara O. *Keepers of the Dream: The Triumph of Effective Schools*. New York: Excelsior, 1994.

Caine, N. Renate, and Caine, Geoffrey. *Making Connections: Teaching and the Human Brain*. Alexandria, Va.: Association for Supervision and Curriculum Development, 1991.

Coleman, J.S., et al. *Equality of Educational Opportunity.* Washington, D.C.: U.S. Office of Education, National Center for Educational Statistics, 1966.

Comer, James. *School Power.* New York: Free Press, 1980.

Dewey, John. *Philosophy, Psychology, and Social Practice.* New York: G.P. Putnam and Sons, 1963.

Duncan, Robert B., and Weiss, Andrew. "Organizational Learning: Implications for Organizational Design." In *Research in Organizational Behavior I,* edited by B. Shaw. Greenwich, Conn.: JAI Press, 1979.

Edmonds, Ronald. "Effective Schools for the Urban Poor." *Educational Leadership* 37 (October 1979): 15-24.

Edmonds, R.R., and Frederickson, J.R. "Search for Effective Schools: The Identification and Analysis of City Schools that Are Instructionally Effective for Poor Children." Manuscript. Center for Urban Studies, Harvard University, Cambridge, Mass., 1978.

Fullan, Michael. "Change Processes and Strategies at the Local Level." *Elementary School Journal* 85 (January 1985): 391-419.

Fullan, Michael. *Change Forces: Probing the Depths of Educational Reform.* London: Falmer Press, 1993.

Fullan, Michael, and Stiegelbauer, Suzanne. *The New Meaning of Educational Change.* New York: Teachers College Press, 1991.

General Accounting Office. *Effective Schools Programs: Their Extent and Characteristics.* Washington, D.C., 1989.

Goodlad, John I. *A Place Called School.* New York: McGraw-Hill, 1984.

Goodlad, John I. *Teachers for Our Nation's Schools.* San Francisco: Jossey-Bass, 1990.

Goodlad, John I. *Educational Renewal: Better Teachers, Better Schools.* San Francisco: Jossey-Bass, 1994.

Huberman, A. Michael, and Miles, Matthew B. "Rethinking the Quest for School Improvement: Some Findings from the DESSI Study." *Teachers College Record* 86 (Fall 1984): 35-54.

Katz, Daniel, and Kahn, Robert. *The Social Psychology of Organizations.* New York: John Wiley and Sons, 1966.

Kouzes, James M., and Posner, Barry Z. *Credibility: How Leaders Gain and Lose It, Why People Demand It.* San Francisco: Jossey-Bass, 1993.

Levine, Daniel U., and Eubanks, Eugene E. "Achievement Improvement and Non-Improvement at Concentrated Poverty Schools in Big Cities." *Metropolitan Education,* November 1986.

Levine, Daniel U., and Eubanks, Eugene E. "Site-Based Management: Engine for Reform or Pipedream? Problems, Pitfalls, and Prerequisites for Success." In *Restructuring the Schools: Problems and Prospects*, edited by J.J. Lane and E.G. Epps. Berkeley, Calif.: McCutchan, 1992.

Lezotte, Lawrence; Miller, Stephen; Hathaway, Douglas; Passalacqua, Joseph; and Brookover, Wilbur. "School Learning, Climate, and Student Achievement." Manuscript. SSTA Center, Florida State University, Tallahassee, 1980.

Marburger, Carl L. *One School at a Time: School-Based Management, A Process for Change*. Columbia, Md.: National Committee for Citizens in Education, 1985.

Morrison, Toni. *The Bluest Eye*. New York: Penguin, 1994.

Muncey, Donna, and McQuillan, Patrick J. *Contested Power and the Negotiation of School Change: An Educational Reform Movement in Anthropological Perspective*. Manuscript. November 1993.

Murray, Charles, and Herrnstein, Richard. *The Bell Curve*. New York: Free Press, 1994.

National Center for Effective Schools Research and Development (NCESRD). *A Conversation Between James Comer and Ronald Edmonds: Fundamentals of Effective Schools Improvement*. Okemos, Mich., 1989.

Negroni, P. "A Case Study in Systemic Reconstruction: The Struggle to Transform the Schools in Springfield, Massachusetts." In *The State of the Nation's Public Schools: A Conference Report*, edited by Stanley Elam. Bloomington, Ind.: Phi Delta Kappa, 1993.

Phi Delta Kappa. *Why Do Some Urban Schools Succeed?* Bloomington, Ind., 1980.

Purkey, Stewart C., and Smith, Marshall S. "Effective Schools: A Review." *Elementary School Journal* 83, no. 4 (1983): 427-52.

Raspberry, William. "Power of Expectations," *Washington Post*, 23 August 1993, p. 17.

Rutter, Michael, et al. *Fifteen Thousand Hours: Secondary Schools and Their Effects on Children*. Cambridge, Mass.: Harvard University Press, 1979.

Schein, Edgar. *Organizational Culture and Leadership*. San Francisco: Jossey-Bass, 1985.

Schlecty, Phillip C. *Schools for the 21st Century*. San Francisco: Jossey-Bass, 1990.

119

Schmoker, Michael J., and Wilson, Richard B. *Total Quality Education: Profiles of Schools that Demonstrate the Power of Deming's Management Principles.* Bloomington, Ind.: Phi Delta Kappa Educational Foundation, 1993.

Schon, Donald A. *The Reflective Practitioner: How Professionals Think in Action.* New York: Basic Books, 1983.

Senge, Peter M. *The Fifth Discipline.* New York: Doubleday Currency, 1990.

Shoemaker, Joan, and Villanova, Robert. *Connecticut Interview and Questionnaire.* Hartford: Connecticut Department of Education, 1983.

Stampen, Jacob O. "Improving the Quality of Education: W. Edwards Deming and Effective Schools." *Contemporary Education Review* 3 (Winter 1987): 423-33.

Taylor, Barbara O. *Implementing What Works: Elementary Principals and School Improvement Programs.* Doctoral dissertation, University Microfilms International #8502445. Northwestern University, 1984.

Taylor, Barbara O., and Levine, Daniel U. "Effective Schools Projects and School-Based Management. *Phi Delta Kappan* 72 (January 1991): 394-97.

Teddlie, Charles, and Stringfield, Samuel. *Schools Make a Difference.* New York: Teachers College Press, 1993.

Tomlinson, T.M. "Student Ability, Student Background, and Student Achievement: Another Look at Life in Effective Schools." Paper presented at Educational Testing Service Conference on Effective Schools, New York, May 1980.

Weber, George. *Inner-City Children Can Be Taught to Read: Four Successful Schools.* Washington, D.C.: Council for Basic Education, 1971.

Weick, K.E. *The Social Psychology of Organizing,* 2nd edition. New York: Addison-Wesley, 1979.

Whitehead, A.N. *Aims of Education and Other Essays.* New York: Macmillan, 1929.

About the Authors

Barbara O. Taylor, working with Beverly Bancroft and Lawrence Lezotte, founded the National Center for Effective Schools Research and Development in 1986. She served as executive director of the center in 1988 and 1989.

A consultant on school reform, school governance, and the management of change, Taylor draws on an extensive background in community planning and development, political lobbying, and program development and implementation in education at the state and local levels.

A graduate of Smith College, Taylor holds a master's degree in management from the J.L. Kellogg School and a Ph.D. in educational administration and policy studies from Northwestern University.

Pamela Bullard is a writer with degrees in law and journalism. She has reported for the *New York Daily News*, the *Newark Star Ledger*, the *Boston Herald*, and the *Boston Herald American*, where she served as education editor during Boston's desegregation crisis.

Bullard also has worked in television as a correspondent, editor, anchorwoman, and producer for WGBH-TV and WCVB-TV in Boston and for PBS. Bullard has served on the faculties of Harvard University, Boston University, and Emerson College.

Bullard's 1980 book, *The Hardest Lesson, Boston's Desegregation Crisis*, co-authored with Judith Stoia, won the American Christopher Award.

Pamela Bullard and Barbara Taylor's previous book together is *Making School Reform Happen*, published by Allyn and Bacon in 1993. That book was reprinted in 1994 by Excelsior with the title, *Keepers of the Dream: The Triumph of Effective Schools*.